The Englishman's Garden

EDITED BY ALVILDE LEES-MILNE AND ROSEMARY VEREY

FOREWORD BY
THE MARCHIONESS OF SALISBURY

DAVID R. GODINE · PUBLISHER · BOSTON

First U.S. edition published in 1983 by
David R. Godine, Publisher, Inc.
306 Dartmouth Street, Boston, Massachusetts 02116

Third printing September 1985

ISBN 0-87923-456-3

LC 82-082733

First published in 1982 by Allen Lane, London

Printed in Great Britain

Contents

Foreword

by The Marchioness of Salisbury

What, I ask myself, is an Englishwoman doing writing a foreword to this book, one moreover, strongly anti-feminist, with very little knowledge of botany or horticulture and without even a smattering of Latin.

Though much flattered to have been asked, I am not sure that the possible answer to this question commends itself to me. Can I hear the cry of 'equal opportunity' echoing through the wilderness? For when the companion book to this volume was published its foreword was written by someone immensely more distinguished and erudite than I, but described by himself as a mere man. However, 'When Adam delved and Eve span, who was then the gentleman?'

My lords and masters, our contributors, are indeed worthy descendants of the gardening Adam, and as I read these pages I felt I had paid a visit to Paradise. Deeply impressed and much humbled by their obvious mastery of gardening in all its aspects and their skilful creation of so much beauty, I found their triumphs in the art of gardening shining through a cloud of modesty.

Alvilde Lees-Milne and Rosemary Verey had the admirable notion of asking no less than thirty-three of these elusive characters to write about their own creations, and though we do not know how hard Adam was meant to have worked in the Garden of Eden (only that he was told to dress it and keep it), it becomes very clear to us as we read this book how hard our contributors have laboured to make and keep in all perfection their particular Edens.

'The pursuit of perfection,' Matthew Arnold said, 'is the pursuit of sweetness and light,' and here in these many gardens the two seem indeed to have been taken captive.

Only a handful of our contributors mention having any help at all, and even fewer that they have a gardener. Yet in spite of this lack of help it is encouraging to note that there is a sturdy trend away from the obsession of giving priority to making the garden labour-free, furnished with plants that create conditions where as far as possible weeds cannot grow. This fashion, if fashion it could be called, tended to lead to a drab and boring uniformity and more seriously to the loss of many beautiful plants and flowers, and to many of these becoming rare, unobtainable or even extinct. It seemed you did not grow the plants and flowers you loved because they made too much work, and gardens were in grave danger of becoming like houses done over by a decorator. Reduce the size of your garden, yes, if this becomes necessary – it is sad but wise – invest in labour-saving tools and devices, mulch, mulch, mulch, and use bricks, gravel, and stone to save labour, but have the plants you love. 'Remember,' said Ruskin, 'that the most beautiful things in the world are the most useless, peacocks and lilies for instance.'

I find it most encouraging that hardly a contributor has mentioned ground-cover, hardly a contributor has mentioned saving labour, and that we find, throughout the accounts they have written of their gardens, an all-pervading love of plants.

It is encouraging, too, that one of the deepest instincts of man, which is to create a garden himself with his own hands, has still such strength. Since earliest times he seems to have had this desire to re-create a Paradise Garden, a Garden of Eden, and in medieval times when he believed in the existence of the Garden, or that it could be made again, the sensible man worked to create his own Paradise, where he could retire within his own walls and, with the door shut upon the wilderness of the disordered world outside, could enjoy, in his *hortus conclusus*, the peace of recreational gardening among the restful plants that bring quietness to a man's spirit. 'True happiness,' said Addison, 'is of a retired nature, and an enemy to pomp and noise.'

Another thing we note as we read this book is that the

hearts of these gardeners are perpetually full of optimism. The disasters of one season will be transformed into the triumphs of the next: disease, decay, the depredations of the weather, destroying frost, drought, flood, tempest, all will be overcome and in another season or another year the perfection of Paradise will be achieved.

But, as I have already mentioned, what comes through to us above all in these pages is the great love with which these gardens and their plants are cherished; though each of the gardeners shows wide diversity of taste and mood there is this one uniting thread which gives us a vivid realization of why the heart of a garden dies with its owner. For once the hand that created it has gone, the magic with which love invested it vanishes. I write this knowing that three of our contributors have died since they wrote their pieces and it is a great sadness that they did not live to see this book published, but we must hope that their gardens will be the exceptions to prove the rule. They have left us their own record of the beauties of their gardens and they will be an added memorial to the memory of three great and skilful gardeners.

When I had finished reading this book, I was left above all with a feeling of encouragement and hope for the future of gardening in England and also with the delightful thought that if it is true, as Jerome K. Jerome said, that 'it is impossible to enjoy idling thoroughly unless one has plenty of work to do' our contributors must be most thoroughly enjoying themselves.

Moreover, how thoroughly this enjoyment is deserved by these thirty-three Englishmen who have followed the noble tradition of other great English gardeners and know, as Macaulay did, that *our* 'acre of Middlesex (or wherever) is better than a principality in Utopia'.

Marjorie Salisbury

Preface

by Alvilde Lees-Milne and Rosemary Verey

The interest shown in our first joint venture, *The English-woman's Garden*, was far greater than we anticipated. So this venture is the answer to the constant question, 'When are you going to do a book on the men?' Realizing that the interest was genuine we set to work. Selecting the gardens has been extremely difficult because we are limited to thirty-three. The choice was great and, as before, the quality was very high. Those chosen are with few exceptions gardens created by their present owners, but inevitably we have had to omit many we would have dearly liked to include.

At first we were unaware what the differences between the men's and women's themes would be. The majority of contributors to *The Englishwoman's Garden* had no professional background, and their lives and their gardens proved to be the successful means of expressing their artistic ability. This is not the case with the men. Many, in fact a third, are indeed professional gardeners, specialists in their own field, be it alpines, trees, garden design or merely the creation of a great garden. We are especially grateful to them for imparting a wealth of horticultural knowledge and garden philosophy, even at times their cherished secrets. These contributors amount to a galaxy of stars.

Another third are connected with the arts in one form or another, and their artistic expertise and keen eye for colour, style and form are clearly visible.

What about the final third? They are men who do not fall into either of the first two categories but just garden because they love it, probably as a complete contrast to their other interests. They too have created exciting gardens.

Both the women and men contributors to these two books share a love of plants and a determination to make their surroundings not only beautiful but interesting. The difference between them comes in their approach to the subject. Generally speaking the men are more serious, definite and self-assured. On the other hand many of the women were agreeably surprised when they found how successful their gardens turned out to be. The men mostly set out with a definite end in view. They are perhaps more practical and less theoretical. They are less impetuous in their gardening and more inclined to look before they leap. They do not rely so much on the process of elimination, although the final result may not necessarily be any better than the women's.

Finally we would like to thank all the contributors for their help and also the several photographers who had to battle with a sunless summer. We do hope that this book will prove as enjoyable and informative as *The Englishwoman's Garden*.

Alvilde Lees-Milne

Rosemary Verey.

All bliss
Consists in this,
To do as Adam did.

Traherne (1637–1674)

The Old School, Langford, Oxfordshire

Hardy Amies's Garden

What fun! I am going to write about my garden. There is only one thing better: that is talking about it and showing people around it. I shall try to do both.

It all started with my sister buying a cottage in a village on the edge of the Cotswolds, bewitching me with the charm of the region and telling me seven years ago that the Old School, built in 1840, was for sale.

One look and I knew what I could do with it. The building was of Cotswold stone, vaguely in the style of the seventeenth century. Behind there was the playground, surrounded by a grey wall. Mercifully there was no asphalt: just an untidy cottage garden. I bought.

What particularly attracted me was the discovery that the sun shone on the garden all day long. Later I realized that this was because the four corners of the garden were the points of the compass. There is therefore no north-facing wall.

The size was roughly fifty-eight feet by fifty-five. I had made a garden in Kensington of the same proportion but half the size. I was determined to benefit by my mistakes made there, but also to repeat and improve on success. I was happy that the new garden had no buildings to cast shadows and that the only trees, yews, were on the north and not in my garden at all, but in my neighbours'.

The making of both gardens brought home to me a simple rule. Where walls are visible, your paths and beds must be straight and related to the walls. You can only permit meandering paths and irregular beds and pools if your background is the sky and trees with their irregular shapes. Was it Miss Jekyll or Vita Sackville-West who said one should aim at formal planning and building in stone or brick and then allow irregular planting to take over? It soon did.

Another rule is that no path should be less than three feet wide. This permits relaxed movement and stops you walking like a geisha. A width of five feet allows you to have a companion and is still better.

I also like symmetry. I suppose it is impossible to be a dress designer and not admire the proportions of the human body. I do, indeed: and symmetry and balance contribute much to its beauty. There are pairs of several things: ears, eyes, arms, bosoms and gentlemen's things which we can't talk about. And where there is anything single, like a nose, a navel or anything still less mentionable, these are bang in the middle. So it has to be with my garden. The site was very irregular. I ignored this and made my plans in accordance with the alignment of French windows in my new dining-room. I set the axis of the garden and took care to have equally sized beds on either side of the main path. The focal point of this is a summerhouse. This I need to provide shade on a summer's day, for the stone paths and the terrace are sometimes too hot.

The terrace had to be wide enough to hold a group of chairs comfortably. Two steps up to it and raised beds gave a variety of levels and avoided monotony.

There was never any question of there being any grass. Lawns must be spacious and rolling: I dislike them cut up into small pieces. But of course there must be greenery to soften the grey stone. I love the dark green of box; I love the orderliness of clipped hedges and pyramids. There is also a hedge of lavender. The late Lord Harcourt gave me a good tip: always clip lavender soon after the flowers fade and do not leave the top flat, it collects snow and ice which damages it. Paths are of York stone and gravel, with one path of cobbles to vary the textures. So much for the background. Now to the flowers.

I loved roses when I was eight. There was a Climbing 'Richmond' (1905) on the wall of my parents' tiny garden in a north London suburb. I couldn't find one and had to be content with climbing 'Crimson Glory' (1935) which seems a good substitute: deep purple red, full shape and heavy scent. I have two 'New Dawns' because they are so reliable. More spectacular but much less sturdy is 'Variegata di Bologna'; a Bourbon easy to train on the wall, but in a wet year the mauve and white striped petals can remain a dead and soggy ball. 'Kathleen Harrop' is an old steady, and 'Caroline Testout' the most beautiful of all. Behind the summerhouse and trained to climb high into the neighbours' yews are *Rosa moschata*, whose scent delights me, and 'Kiftsgate', which time will probably prove to be too

1. Obelisks and the summerhouse designed by Hardy Amies are built of local Taynton stone. In a garden without trees the summerhouse provides the only shade on hot summer days. Each pillar is generously clothed with climbing roses and clematis.

ambitious. The colours around the walls of pink mauve and deep red are satisfactory; but I'm never sure of the magenta-ish 'Malaga'. On the pillar of the summerhouse and in full sunshine most of the day 'Gloire de Dijon' gives yeoman service from May till November; and on another pillar is the beautiful greeny-white rose called Climbing 'Sombreuil'. On the south-east-facing wall of the house I have two old reliables, 'Mermaid' and 'Madame Alfred Carrière'.

It's not roses, roses all the way: for amongst them on the walls are the beautiful double mauve *Clematis* 'Vyvyan Pennell' and the handsome mauve *C.* 'Lasurstern'. There are also two *Actinidia kolomikta* and in the sunniest corner, a fig.

Very important is a *Clematis spooneri*: I love the bold simple statement of the petals. Almost better is *C. montana grandiflora*. Equally cherished are two honeysuckles, one which scents the summerhouse and another which climbs into my bedroom. I have yet to find a scent better than that of *Lonicera periclymenum* 'Belgica'. So much for the drapery of the walls.

I would love to have filled the two rose beds with old-fashioned bush roses. Bunyard's book, published in 1936, was a great revelation to me. That, and my friendship with John Fowler, started my interest in old flowers. John truly taught me to have taste in flowers. It was no longer the biggest and brightest but the most subtle.

The Austin roses are exactly what they say they are. The flowers have the shape, colour and scent of old roses, with the perpetual flowering habits of the floribunda. In each bed I had to include a 'Rosa Mundi' bush which I keep well clipped. Also a moss or two; and I struggle with 'Souvenir du Dr Jamain'. For steady flowering all season long I have 'Yvonne Rabier', 'Grüss an Aachen' and 'Natalie Nypels'.

The four centrally planted standards are 'The Fairy': a tiny mistake. 'The Fairy' has just a touch of salmon in its pink which is maddening. Another time I would choose 'Ballerina', which is a clearer pink, or 'Little White Pet'.

The jump to the front garden completes the rose story. It would seem that the stone walls of the School House are much liked by *Rosa banksiae* 'Lutea' double yellow. Mine oblige with a dazzling early display. I keep them clipped hard against the wall, in spite of the warnings that they should not be pruned.

A longer display is given by a pleasant-shaped little white single rose, growing in clusters, with a musk smell, called 'Trier'. Ground cover for the two main rose beds is provided by cranesbill and species of geraniums. I had to thin out the vigorous ones. They must love the lime for they soon smother the roses. I encourage the low-growers and spreaders like *G. sangineum lancastriense, G. dalmaticum, G. subcaulescens,* and *G. tuberosum*. A favourite is *G. phaeum*, the dark purple widow geranium.

For my business I have to travel a lot. But it would have to be something very important to keep me away from my garden at Easter and in June. I am usually away in February and March – missing, alas, the first excitements of the spring, but usually giving me time enough to be back for most of the daffodils and the tulips.

I am calmly extravagant about tulips. I want the two main rose beds to be packed with them. Deep purple to striped white and pink are the colours for the rose beds; and yellow for the front garden.

I should love to make an all-yellow garden. It is a colour perfect for the Cotswolds, with its seventeenth-century traditions and architecture. Wallflowers, Crown Imperials (I have them amongst the yellow tulips), sunflowers, Black-Eyed Susan, all marigolds (very John Gerard!), especially those pretty *Tagetes*. You cannot grow these coloured flowers with anything pink or mauve: they look hideous. Once I had planted a lavender hedge, all yellow and orange things were out.

I despise little herb gardens. There are not enough plants to be useful in the kitchen; and there is no room for the large handsome ones like fennel, lovage, Sweet Cicely and *Angelica*. I now have a bed of mint about four feet by six and a bed of parsley. Fennel grows in a border and variegated mint climbs along the base of the stone wall. My favourite herb is tarragon. I really am good at growing it and am congratulated on its vigour by my grand gardening neighbours. Tarragon needs moist, well-drained soil, protection from wind and a sunlit aspect. You have to plant it on a site which suits it rather than in a spot which suits you. You must clip it constantly, just snipping off the first shoots when the plant is a foot high. It disappears completely in winter, but will survive even the hardest frosts. It hates neglect and if allowed to grow free and untouched will lose its savour, its leaves turning grey and dull, like its cousin the mugwort. Tarragon (*Artemisia dracunculus*) should have dark shiny leaves. Every two years you should split the roots neatly into two and replant both parts. This seems to revitalize the pungency, which is essential. It is often said that the tarragon plant, often called French Tarragon, reverts to Russian Tarragon. This of course is nonsense. It is just the results of neglect. Six plants give me enough to make tarragon vinegar and to give bunches to visiting friends.

From an interest in herbs, I quickly moved to aromatics. As my garden is small there must be more to interest the visitor than just by the eye. The nose comes into play – *Lippia citriodora, Perovskia, Caryopteris*, all get their leaves pinched as we go by.

The main layout of stone, pebble, box and lavender hedges was completed and mature before I caught on to alpines.

2. A view from a corner of the garden where seats placed to catch the sun are surrounded by sweet-smelling shrubs such as lavender and thyme.

One visit to Joe Elliott at Broadwell was enough to fire me. I grow the hardy ones, the easy saxifrages like the small campanulas, in two rows on either side of the main path. Joe Elliott calls it my alpine herbaceous border! As alpines flower at various seasons and many have attractive foliage, there is fun all the year round. Miniature spring bulbs like the Petticoat Daffodil are mixed in. I keep the woody ones lightly clipped (little and often is my motto for all my box, myrtles and yews), then there is room for more alpines at the base of the stone walls supporting beds and terrace.

The front door is flanked by two white daphnes and one *D. mezereum*. The double white *Clematis* 'Duchess of Edinburgh' is a real success. I have optimistically planted a *Magnolia grandiflora*. Between the gravel path and the stone wall along the street, there is a really handsome hedge of rosemary, which is kept well trimmed too.

The School House garden, both back and front, has a formal layout, but it is a cottage garden, with more to do with a *potager du curé* than with a parterre. I have flowers all the year round, with an accent on spring and summer; but I cannot cope seriously with the autumn in such a small place. Each plant is named as carefully and correctly as I can manage. This is a good training for me: I love the history of plants. If I could plan my life again I would love to study botany and of course Latin.

I should like to say something positive and I hope helpful, particularly to future makers of small gardens, especially those in the suburbs of London, which is where I came from. You should never be frightened of making a small garden formal. Many people think a formal garden is something grand. A classically planned – and that means a naturally planned – cottage garden has a path straight from the gate up to the front door, with beds on either side; or two grass plots with paths and beds outlining the walls. Totally harmonious and ready for any mixture you choose. You must submit to the formality of the shape of the walls. You will then have peace and harmony and very often style.

Hardy Amies

3 (*above right*). The box-edged symmetry of Hardy Amies's garden is apparent in this aerial view. The honey-coloured Cotswold stone wall surrounding the garden makes a perfect foil for Hardy Amies's carefully chosen colour schemes.

4. Every available space in the gardens is used to advantage. Here Rock Roses and *Dianthus* spill over the low stone wall.

Chandos Lodge, Eye, Suffolk

Sir Frederick Ashton's Garden

I bought Chandos Lodge about twenty-five years ago. I bought it for the house, not for the land, the amount of which, about eight or nine acres, horrified me. How on earth was I going to cope with all that, I thought, having come from a tiny cottage with only a patch of ground. My sister said, 'Don't be so stupid. Of course you will manage somehow.' Although I was born in Ecuador and lived in Peru, I suppose I gravitated to Suffolk because it was where my mother came from.

Initially I knew practically nothing about gardening except the little I had learnt from my cottage garden at Yaxley, near Eye. In the beginning I used to order one of everything since I imagined things would spread. It took me a long time to get into the habit of ordering two, three or four of any one plant.

When I arrived here the garden looked very different from what it does now. There was an enormous rockery and terrible arbours covered with weeds of every description. I planned the garden progressively, never having any professional advice. However, I did have a friend, Martyn Thomas, who was a marvellous gardener. Later on he helped me tremendously.

I had no particular scheme in mind. I began by sitting and looking and getting into a kind of state. I suppose in a sense I did a certain amount of choreography, starting without being quite sure what I was going to do, and with rather congested thoughts. Suddenly things fell into shape. My ballet work influenced me a lot. I was repeating my thoughts with the plants. I put them like the dancers into what I thought the right places and then moved them about. I have no compunction about that. If a thing is six inches out I have to move it until it is absolutely right for my eye. This to me is terribly important. It is rather like doing a stage décor.

I am a great one for flying in the face of nature, believing you can grow everything you want – even indoor plants outside. Oddly enough it sometimes works.

When planting I used to get someone to stand with sticks to be moved about. I would go far away, saying, 'More to the left, or the right!' Then, 'That's all right. Put it there!' Even then things often got moved again. When I sit on the terrace with my drink I like to suppose that everything is in the right place.

I am not passionately keen on strong colours in a garden, particularly a lot of red. I like muted colours, such as pale yellows, greens and variegated-leaved plants. Most of my ideas have come from books and, although I have not seen many French gardens, I have always had a feeling for them. I know Versailles of course but not Vaux-le-Vicomte. Yet I feel I know so many of them from studying the wonderful books I have. I first came to hear of Le Nôtre when Sachie Sitwell said I looked exactly like him, I don't know why. But after that I began to look at his gardens. I loved them – all that formality greatly appeals to me. Of course when I laid out the formal part here I didn't scale it properly. Little yew trees arrived about a foot high, and now they are all on top of each other. I clearly do not have Le Nôtre's sense of space.

I also bought masses of little box plants to create the topiary. Some of the golden box I think I got as cuttings when at Chatsworth years ago. I adore every kind of box. It smells delicious. I even have a so-called weeping variety. I had seen it in Battersea Park and was determined to get one. Unfortunately with me it only seems to be a horizontal grower. Sometimes when friends ask me what I think of their gardens I say, 'You are over-conifered.' Well, of course, I am over-boxed and yewed.

I am also very fond of golden privet. I used to take cuttings of this from the square gardens when walking from my house in London to Kensington tube station. I now have it

5 (*above*). Poised like a dancer on a stage, a statue is placed strategically in a green vista framed by clipped yews.

6 (*below*). A stage crowded with clipped yews and box dancers shows the hand of the master choreographer.

along a path clipped into squares and balls, and from a distance it looks surprisingly good as it catches the light.

I particularly like statues in a garden. So I bought a lot of cheapish ones, and if they looked too bad I covered them with ivy, of which I am very fond. They use it a lot in America; and on tours there with the ballet I used to visit some of those lovely gardens and take notes. I have made several animals of various ivies on wire frames – hedgehogs, ducks and pigs. It is fun to do and they look pretty.

But I don't much care for borders and beds. I inherited one huge border. I dug up all the things I didn't like, lupins, delphiniums and so forth, put a box hedge round it and filled it with day lilies and a few other favourites. I can't grow azaleas and rhododendrons, which doesn't worry me. Somebody once gave me a hideous red rhododendron. I put it in the driest part of the garden, hoping it would die. Not a bit of it.

My favourite shrubs are the *Daphne* family, but like one's friends they suffer from sudden death. One day they are very beautiful, and the next they are gone. I have many old roses, but I also love 'La France' and 'Madame Abel Chatenay', and the double yellow Banksian rose with that wonderful, slightly violet smell does very well in spite of the cold winds and is, I think, my favourite.

In the beginning I bought all my roses from a north-country nursery where they were not grown on their own roots, and when I came back from a Royal Ballet tour in America there were so many suckers flowering that I almost had an Alexandra Rose Day garden, which wasn't bad.

I love small plants and wild flowers such as buttercups and daisies, aconites and snowdrops, cowslips, and those tiny wild daffodils you see in Cumbria. Elaborate plants don't appeal to me.

I have a theory that every garden should have certain trees, a walnut, a medlar, a quince, a Cedar of Lebanon, a mulberry and a fig. All of these I planted. I put the cedar plumb in the middle of what used to be a tennis court, where after twenty years it is now spreading out beautifully. Another thing I believe to be essential, if one can possibly have it, is water. I did a television programme of one of my ballets called *La Fille mal gardée*, and put all the money that I earned into digging a huge hole simply to have water. There was a small spring which is now a fair-sized pond surrounded with primulas. I think that another of my ballets called *The Dream* would look lovely in this setting and I sometimes say to myself that if only I had enough money, what fun it would be to give a party and get the *corps de ballet* down here.

What I have enjoyed most is planning the garden and watching it grow. My advice to beginners would be, 'Do exactly what you want to do, and don't listen to anybody.' Being a compulsive gardener that is what I did. I studied the land and went ahead from that. Put in the plants you like. And if you like those terrible red salvias then put them in.

7. The pyramids and dwarf hedges surround a pedestal topped by a stone urn. The standard box balls give enviable shape and height, emphasizing the drama of this corner.

8. The variety of shapes and the evergreen contrasts of colour and texture ensure that this is a garden for all seasons. Carefully directed clipping is of vital importance.

9. Along the path to the gothic folly a line of stern box balls glower at the one surviving herbaceous border planted with drifts of delphiniums, Day Lilies and other favourite flowers.

10. Hostas in variety encircle a stone urn. A bower supporting a white clematis repeats the motif of the gothic glazing bars. The vibrant pink-washed walls of house and garden buildings provide a perfect backdrop.

Now, owing to age, various infirmities and lack of help I have no more projects. Sometimes I see a weed at my feet and it may be days before I can make the effort to get it out. I only use weed-killer on paths. Otherwise it is hand-weeding, or no weeding at all.

I think more and more people are taking to gardening to get away from the horrors of life. At least in the garden there is peace. All I need is no interruptions. What I really welcome is a postal strike.

Frederick Ashton

Old Rectory Cottage, Tidmarsh, Berkshire

Bill Baker's Garden

A shooting man had lived here, definitely a non-gardener. The hedges were twenty feet high, a few runner beans in one corner, otherwise nothing but jungle. Even so, we were thrilled to find a cottage surrounded by its own meadows, bordered by a chalk stream and having an old orchard with a silted-up lake. The possibilities were considerable and a wild garden was inevitable, but that was more than twenty-five years ago.

That first winter we attacked the undergrowth with the help of a hedge-laying old-age pensioner and five Wessex sows. A bucket of pignuts thrown into a bramble thicket quickly demolished it, while ground elder was dug up and eaten with relish. With an electric fence and the pigs every inch of the ground was covered and not a blade of grass left.

While the pigs were doing their stuff I was drawing plans. I wanted an informal cottage garden with grass paths surrounding island beds, all designed for ease of mowing. The problem of edging, which is about as tedious as mowing, I solved by making a right-angle strip of concrete which does not show, my inspiration being an article in the *Gardener's Chronicle*. Labour-saving ideas are most important, for I do all the work. Each grass path had a purpose, leading to an aviary, or our special dogs' garden, or even a seat, so necessary for the weary gardener.

Foliage colours, shape and textures are of great importance to any garden, equally so the correct placing and proportion of evergreens for winter effect. So the next step was to plan mixed shrub borders to produce a backcloth of gold, purple, grey or variegated. This has been most successful, especially when using a bright red climbing rose to scramble into the Weeping Silver-Leaved Pear (*Pyrus salicifolia* 'Pendula'), the purple *Clematis jackmanii* 'Superba' into the yellow-foliaged *Laburnum* and the rather unusual combination of *Lathyrus grandiflorus* scrambling through *Cornus* 'Elegantissima'.

A very early priority was the rock garden, sited on each side of the main path for ease of access. It was required as a home for alpines collected from such far-away mountains as the Atlas or the Caucasus, or wheresoever my annual pilgrimage had taken me. It also helped with the disposal of great heaps of builders' rubble which were buried underneath. Eight hand-made sinks, two with lime-free soil and one made of tufa blocks, house the less aggressive alpines.

The rock garden, being the only well-drained place in the garden, grows the wild crocus extremely well. *Crocus aureus* seeds everywhere so that in February, with *Iris histrioides*, it is at its most colourful. But every month has its flower – even November will see *Galanthus corcyrensis* and *Cyclamen coum* braving our weather.

As my soil is a limy clay I planned two peat beds, one in the sun and one in the shade. This was partly in order to grow the Asiatic gentians, but they refused to flower in the shade and dried up and died in the sun. However, dodecatheons love the sunny one and choice ferns the shady one, so I'm quite content.

Another habitat I wanted to produce was a small bog garden and it was easily contrived by burying an old polythene haystack-cover two feet underground near the overflow of a small pool. Here *Iris kaempferi* grew for a number of years until the lime seeped in, but the Sensitive Fern (*Onoclea sensibilis*) with several dentarias still survives. The pool itself manages one water-lily, an *Iris laevigata*, and lots of frogs descended from a blob of frog-spawn introduced long ago.

Island beds were needed to house my ever-growing collection of plants, often gifts from other gardening friends now passed on. Frequently I am torn between the desire to put a plant where it will grow best or where it will look best. Occasionally it works both ways, an example being the

rounded leaves of the Birthwort (*Aristolochia clematitis*) coming up round the spiky yucca. In another bed the grey-green leaves of a wandering euphorbia collected in Yugoslavia have surrounded a tree ivy, produced from a cutting of a flowering shoot, and look just right.

Being at the bottom of a valley means that we are in a dreadful frost pocket, so the shelter given by the cottage and stable walls is even more valuable than usual. Every wall is covered with climbers and wall shrubs, the annual pruning being a major and very necessary operation. We rescued a venerable and tangled wisteria in the early days, but it now has to share its wall with the evergreen *Euonymus fortunei* and the golden-foliaged *Jasminum nudiflorum* 'Aureum', so catering for winter months.

On the sunny side of the cottage we had planted a *Tecoma* and a Banksian rose whose yellow flowers used to mingle with the wisteria, but the 1979 winter seemed even worse than '63 and we lost them both. Quickly the variegated jasmine and a *Clematis campaniflora* took advantage of their going and at the end of a year every space was filled. At the back of the cottage it is very shady, ideal for *Parthenocissus henryana* and a *Chaenomeles* with three clumps of mistletoe growing on it.

Another casualty of 1979 was *Solanum jasminoides*, which, after a mild winter, would go right over the stable roof. Its neighbour, *Clematis durandii*, had rather a hard time, although the combination of blue and white flowers was very pleasing.

Nearby is a *Ceanothus thyrsiflorus repens*, forced to stand upright against a wall, but it is the only evergreen *Ceanothus* which is hardy with us. Under it is planted my favourite clematis, the deep pink *C. texensis* hybrid 'Étoile Rose', which enjoys both the support and the protection it receives. Small-flowered clematis don't get the deadly clematis wilt and are perfect for growing over small trees and shrubs. *Clematis alpina* 'Columbine' has the silvery leaves of *Cystisus battandieri* to blend with its pale blue flower, while elsewhere *Clematis macropetala* covers and flowers at the same time as an amelanchier. Later the fluffy seed heads of this clematis are attractive; even better are those of the orange-peel form of *C. orientalis*, excelling even our Old Man's Beard (*C. vitalba*).

Under each window I planted a scented shrub. *Daphne odora* has a superb perfume, but *D. bholua* has both scent and a large flower out for quite three months. I must confess to a great weakness for daphnes – there are nine in the rock garden alone and as many again elsewhere.

12. The grass path leading towards the river is flanked by island beds. Here, in June, the graceful and sweetly scented flower sprays of *Buddleja alternifolia* are an important feature.

13. Abundantly filled stone troughs alongside fragrant-leafed *Geranium macrorrhizum* which encircles a dwarf golden yew.

Perhaps it is time to leave the garden around the cottage and explore the wild garden. This part was not planned, but evolved, and now consists of log-edged grass paths winding in and out of trees down to the river. A path under a small brick archway covered with the winter-flowering honeysuckle (*Lonicera fragrantissima*) takes one to an aged mulberry tree whose weighty limbs are chained together for support. Here old apple trees are festooned with clematis, roses and vines of the more vigorous kind. The rose 'Francis E. Lester' is superb, reaching a tremendous height and simply covered with its single pink scented flowers. Fortunately it is not as rampageous as 'Kiftsgate' which actually killed its poor tree. Single roses look best in the wild garden and my preference for them is shown in a hedge planted with the cream single Scots Rose *Rosa pimpinellifolia* 'Hispida'.

In early spring the inviting vistas of the river are enhanced by drifts of crocus, aconites and snowdrops. Hellebores add to the scene and are followed by wild daffodils which I am trying to naturalize. In damper places *Fritillaria meleagris* and *Leucojum aestivum* are happily seeding about and even put up with flooding. Willows of many varieties provide catkins of different colour in early spring and under them grow candelabra primulas and water-loving iris. Damp is really quite an advantage, but extra humus is also necessary and this is supplied in the form of ample top-dressing of horse manure and rotted sawdust first used in the stables as bedding. *Meconopsis* seed into this rich peat-like substance and all the American and Japanese woodlanders like it, as do the colour forms of our own wood anemones.

Summer is just as exciting as the springtime, because now my lilies, which are my great passion, take the stage. One cannot have too many lilies. I grow them in quantities from seed; they are all beautiful and especially dear to me for I arranged their marriages, so they are my children.

The autumn is even more colourful, for now the *Sorbus* avenue in the lane approaching the cottage blazes away. The small island on my lake is also planted for autumn colour, following a profusion of flowers from *Rosa* 'Paulii' and an enormous *R. filipes*. Autumn's chief delight is undoubtedly the hardy cyclamen under all the shrubs, weaving a carpet first of flowers and then of intricately patterned leaves.

But the seasons keep passing and perhaps the wheel has turned full circle, for the garden with its roses and clematis and vines hanging from the trees is but another kind of jungle. The pigs are replaced by Paraquat and the only labour force is once again an old-age pensioner – myself!

Bill Baker

14. A fine specimen of *Parrotia persica*, the cut-leafed Stag's Horn Sumach, *Rhus typhina* 'Laciniata' and *Viburnum opulus* make a bold planting.

15. Every month has its special flowers in the well-drained rock garden in front of the house. Early June is a time for *Dianthus*, dwarf hypericums and hardy geraniums. The harvest of Bill Baker's annual pilgrimage abroad makes this rock garden an alpine enthusiast's paradise.

Hergest Croft Gardens, Kington, Herefordshire

Lawrence Banks's Garden

A great gale blew at Hergest on 1 January 1976 and one of the casualties was an old oak. A count of the rings proved it to have been planted in 1814, the year in which Richard Banks came to Kington. Richard, who was a lawyer, came from Ashford in Kent. According to family tradition the family business of smuggling on Romney Marsh had suffered from the attentions of the Royal Navy after Trafalgar and an alternative profession had to be sought. The law seemed an obvious solution. A certain James Crummer, his uncle by marriage, was the first improver of the future Hergest Croft gardens.

James was a man of taste. He planted a series of windbreaks from the edge of Hergest Ridge down to Ridgebourne, the original house on the property, and some magnificent beeches still stand. But in my mind his memorial is the massive sycamore which now dominates the centre of the garden, a living reproach to those who despise sycamore. James may well have gardened at Ridgebourne itself and the terraces in the style of Repton may be part of his garden. His other horticultural legacy is his gardening books, including the earliest volumes of Curtis's *Botanical Magazine*.

My great-grandfather, Richard William Banks, was the first member of the family to live at Ridgebourne and a number of splendid trees survive from his planting. This garden is dominated by a huge scarred veteran specimen of Greek Fir (*Abies cephalonica*) planted in 1867 to commemorate the birth of his son, William Hartland. This tree, twisted by the great ice storm of 1940 and torn by many a gale, demonstrates that some conifers can still be graceful in old age; it shows every sign of being with us for a long time yet. In 1967 we added another tree of the same species to carry on the tradition and to mark the birth of his great-great-grandson. One other tree of his planting gives me particular pleasure because it was one of the first which I satisfactorily identified for myself, having found it in his planting notebooks; it is the tansy-leaved thorn (*Crataegus tanacetifolia*), which is tucked into a small planting just opposite the front gate, a small tree with tessellated bark and attractive silvery grey foliage, though the orange haws mentioned in Hillier never seem to achieve much colour.

On his marriage in 1894, my grandfather moved up the hill, built a new house and began the creation of a most remarkable garden. He got his priorities clearly in order and started gardening before building his house. His garden grew steadily and by about 1912 he was also planting in a woodland valley half a mile away. The garden today shows his vision and genius and I can only pick out some pieces which give me particular pleasure.

One of the most surprising features is that, apart from a fairly narrow terrace immediately to the south of the house, he did not surround himself with great displays of colour. They are there, but at a distance. Around the lawn, which was a double tennis court, he created a visual concerto mainly from evergreen trees and shrubs – among the most effective combinations are an *Ilex* × *altaclarensis* and a Golden Scots Pine flanked by an upright Irish Yew; the contrasts of colour, form and texture in winter are pure magic. Across the lawn there is a balancing spring group, a Blue Atlantic Cedar skirted with the low golden yew, *Taxus baccata aurea*, which retains its colour all year round, and accented by the acid-yellow leaves of the golden Japanese Maple, *Acer japonicum* 'Aureum'. The deciduous trees in this tapestry of foliage play their part as well, a cut-leaved beech complementing its weeping brother and a vase-shaped *Acer palmatum* 'Senkaki' drawing the eye out to the park beyond, a joy at any time of the year. I treasure a dramatic memory of this tree, with its coral twigs shining in winter sunshine against a backdrop of blackest thunder clouds.

William's range of planting skills was immense. He was as good on the large canvas of parkland and woodland as on the more intimate groups. He took the eighteenth-century tradition of Brown and used it to create a twentieth-century parkland landscape of exotic species which he blended into the Herefordshire countryside without a jarring note. He had his problems and failures, and usually for unexpected reasons: he laid out a great avenue of conifers stretching westwards from the house up the hill. His friends laughed at him and called it the avenue of crates, but the problem now is that the trees have grown so well that the vista up the avenue is obscured.

Two plant pictures in particular show his dramatic use of colour: a rhododendron 'fall' cascading down a steep bank, starting with the fierce pink 'Cynthia' at the top, through 'Mrs E. C. Sterling' and dark-eyed 'Sappho' to the red of 'Doncaster' at the bottom; and lower down the wood, a subtle combination of purple and mauve rhododendrons with the common yellow azalea, one of the rare exceptions to the rule that rhododendrons and azaleas are best kept apart.

After my grandfather's death in 1930 his widow continued with the garden, until she died in 1937. The garden then spent a period as a sleeping beauty until my father returned to live there in 1954. It was well cared for by a devoted head gardener but no new initiatives were taken.

When my father arrived restoration and re-creation were the first priority: the cutting and moving of plants which had been blurred by almost thirty years of growth. Family and gardeners spent many hours of toil dragging forty-year-old plants to new positions where they could develop unobstructed. We found in the process that my grandfather's assessment of the micro-climate of the wood had been accurate; when we moved some early-flowering plants into certain areas, unplanted for no apparent reason, we found that they caught the spring frosts. Such work in a garden such as Hergest is unobtrusive but vital to continue the blend of spectacle and plantsmanship. Nearer home, in Ridgebourne garden, which is a mixture of Victorian vegetable garden and more modern borders, my father's deft touch with plants is more obvious; there is a small pergola covered on one side with *Clematis macropetala* 'Maidwell Hall', a gift from Elliot Hodgkin, who gave us so many good plants, the clearest of blues in May and with woolly seed heads in autumn, intertwining on the other side with John Treasure's form of *Clematis orientalis*, with its lemon-peel flowers. Under the avenue of old apple trees which divides the garden a spring border has evolved. Something was always there but it has thickened over the years and is a joy from the first primulas of March to the columbines of May. A particular delight is a pure red *Anemone fulgens*, with the black centre and no annular ring round it, a plant which

16. Massed rhododendrons in full bloom surge towards the lake in early summer.

17. Glimpsed over the top of the rhododendron 'fall' a shaft of sunlight catches the fresh green growth of the broad-leaved trees surrounding the lake below.

seems to have disappeared from commerce but has survived here for seventy years or more.

The main borders against the terraces at Hergest Croft have encouraged us to venture into half-hardy plants and though winters such as 1978–9 tempt one to give up such foolish optimism we are constantly surprised by what we can grow. This may ironically be due in part to the fact that we are a late garden, which does not tempt plants into early growth only to be savaged by spring frosts. We have established a collection of *Cistus*, which is an interest of mine and which do well with us, though it is wise to keep a reserve stock in the greenhouse.

I have only written about bits of what is a garden of infinite variety, full of charm at any time of the year, from the naturalized *Scilla bifolia* on the lawn in the low February sun as I write, to the pure gold of the Golden Ash, *Fraxinus excelsior* 'Jaspidea', in the mists of October. Every time I walk around I marvel at my forebears' vision and hope to do a little to add to it.

Lawrence Banks

18. Looking up at the rhododendron 'fall' the pink *Rhododendron* 'Cynthia', at the summit, gives way to *R.* 'Mrs E. C. Stirling' and dark-eyed *R.* 'Sappho' to the crimson scarlet of *R.* 'Doncaster' at the bottom.

19. Formal golden and darker green yews protect the croquet lawns. Deciduous trees provide a spectacular backdrop.

20. The twin herbaceous borders give visual interest to the vegetable gardens.

Hungerdown House, Seagry, Wiltshire

Egbert Barnes's Garden

In this garden aconites, *Eranthis hyemalis*, provide our earliest flowers, concentrated under a large Horse Chestnut, then, of course, leafless. Varying in season from January to early March, numbers have been up from natural increase by spreading the corms after flowering. Nearby, snowdrops have also been increased by annually spreading the seedlings.

Next to flower are the species crocus in the orchard: *Crocus tomasinianus*, *C. sieberi*, followed by *C. etruscus*, all from southern Europe, which, by the unaided seeding of the 'Tomasinis', form a sheet of pale mauve. They are succeeded by groups of early narcissus. The trunk of a large oak is encircled by hybrids of *Crocus chrysanthus* planted in groups of many colours. Not long after begins the season of the Japanese Cherries in the cherry walk, an important feature in the design of the garden by Percy Cane, about whose work in England and America and on the Continent much has already been written. To him we owe a great debt for providing the masterly design for us to furnish in succeeding years. Sadly, the cherries are now, after forty years, reaching the end of their natural life's span and some have already been replaced. My favourites are *Prunus sargentii*, *P. serrulata pubescens*, *P. serrulata longipes* and *P. 'Ukon'*. They are underplanted with a carpet of *Anemone apeninna*. Planted as pure blue they are gradually being overtaken by the white form.

The walk leads uphill and from there there is a long vista of lawns, the first framed with Silver Birches and a Weeping Silver Pear, *Pyrus salicifolia pendula*, free-standing in the grass. We have planted one long bed with white, silver and gold – several *Philadelphus*, Rose 'Stanwell Perpetual', *Rubus cockburnianus* (dwarf form) and at their feet Fair Maids of France. Among the gold are *Laburnum 'Vossii'*, *Hypericum 'Elstead'* and *Physocarpus opulifolius 'Luteus'*. This colour note is continued by two sheets of gold on a terrace wall, Mount

Etna Brooms, *Genista aetnensis*, grown as tall standard trees, so light in foliage that they cast no shade on *Alstroemeria ligtu* hybrids beneath.

We have a scarlet bed devoted to bright reds, orange and hard yellows which would not blend with the soft pinks and blues. Here the chief feature is the rose 'Scarlet Fire', climbing through a purple-leaved maple backed by a 'John Downie' crab. Opposite this is a *Buddleja alternifolia* grown as a standard with a trunk of six feet and a span of twenty-three feet. It shares a border with *Mahonia 'Charity'* and winter-flowering, lime-tolerant heaths.

Clematis stray through and over many shrubs. Perhaps the most successful are *C. 'The President'* in the vine *Vitis 'Brant'* on the wall of the house and *C. 'Lasurstern'* in the species lilac, *Syringa × henryi*. How often one reads that a clematis like 'Nellie Moser' should be planted in the shade where it will not fade. Don't believe it. Here she occupies the north-facing angle of the house where not a gleam of sun can reach it and the flowers fade just as quickly as they do anywhere else. On the wall above it *C. armandii* flowers well but is spoilt to my mind by its habit of hanging on to its dead leaves.

A mistake I made was in replacing 100 yards of moribund hedging with laurustinus. The effect is good but it needs a lot of attention in spring at a time when every moment in the garden is precious. In times of frost, when salt is used on the road, the evergreen leaves are often damaged.

When we first came to Hungerdown, in 1936, there was little flower garden, only the two large oaks, once hedgerow trees, a Copper Beech, the orchard, tennis court and privet hedges in plenty. Most of what is now lawns and flowers was then vegetable garden. Planting has gone on steadily each year since the war, until recently when advancing years and reduction in staff have curtailed it. An exception has been

21 (*above*). The gardens of Hungerdown House, designed in the 1930s by Percy Cane for Egbert Barnes, have evolved into a place of great beauty.

22 (*below*). The gateway from the drive to the south-facing terrace is flanked by mellow brick walls and borders well filled with foliage plants.

23. A more recent creation was the garden close by the house, with paths wide enough to accommodate his wife's wheelchair and beds raised high enough to enable her to enjoy her own garden.

24. An important axial feature of the garden is the circular pond with its well-proportioned fountain. Walking down from the terrace we see slopes suitably clothed with bold foliage plants. From here there is a fine view over the Wiltshire countryside.

the little 'arboretum' which came into being in 1962 by the addition of a small paddock. Already established was a Dawn Redwood tree, *Metasequoia glyptostroboides*, one of the earliest seedlings, although not in the original plantings in Britain of the 'living fossil' introduced from China in 1948. There is also a sizeable Swamp Cypress, and, chosen for its graceful shape, is the Serbian Spruce, *Picea omorika*, and two alders, *Alnus glutinosa* and *A. cordata*. Among those chosen for autumn colour are *Liquidambar, Parrotia* and maples, the crab *Malus tschonoskii* and perhaps among the most showy of all, with their berries and coloured leaves, are *Sorbus* 'Embley' and *S.* 'Joseph Rock', which is distinguished by amber berries.

At a later date a small paved area, with low walls and troughs planted chiefly with alpines, was constructed for my wife's wheelchair gardening.

The courtyard is large enough to have its corners rounded off by my beloved cyclamen, *Cyclamen hederifolium*, flowering from August to December in two corners; *C. coum*, flowering December to April, in the other two. There can be few plants easier to grow and more rewarding than *C. hederifolium*. A double handful of leaf mould enriched with the J.I. base worked into the limestone chippings, and top dressing of the same each year when dormant, will furnish all they desire but surely less than they deserve for a show in flowers or patterned leaves or both for almost ten months of the year. Experts now tell us to plant them 'in the green'. This is good for the plants and suits me too, because, with the leaves there, I cannot plant the corms upside down. Above the latter in the northern corner we planted, in 1950, an Arizona Cypress, *Cupressus arizonica*, far too big for its station, but who could grudge such a beautiful tree all the space it needs? In the corner diagonally opposite, where it never gets a ray of sunshine, we planted *Camellia* 'J. C. Williams'. In 1973 it could be measured in inches and now scales six feet. Tree peonies lend distinction to the other two corners: *P. suffruticosa* to the one; 'Mrs Kelway', a gorgeous white, to the other.

Ground coverers are always being talked about. My vote in the 'best of all' class would be for the evergreen *Geranium macrorrhizum*, especially in its white-flowered form. Its dying leaves assume bright autumn colours. The plant is not deep-rooting like *Tellima grandiflora*, which must I think count in its favour, but the latter is certainly effective and is also evergreen.

Egbert Barnes.

26. The main glade, designed by Percy Cane, is punctuated by Silver Birches, their white trunks a special feature in winter.

Walpole House, Chiswick Mall, London W4

Jeremy Benson's Garden

Walpole House lies by the Thames with only a road, Chiswick Mall, and a narrow strip of garden between it and the river. Fifty yards out is Chiswick Eyot – a long low mud-covered gravel bank on which grow close-cropped willows – and beyond is the broad curve of Chiswick Reach. From street level it is the houses and their narrow riverside gardens that dominate the scene, but from the higher levels it is the views out over the river that count. There could hardly be a better place in which to live and work.

Walpole, unlike the adjoining houses, has no garden at all on the river's edge – we thank our good neighbours who own and look after the strip across our frontage. But Walpole does have an unfairly large L-shaped garden behind; for London, the garden is huge – two-thirds of an acre.

Both my wife and I are architects, so for us much of the pleasure in any garden lies in its plan, its lines and levels, and the way in which the spaces fit together. Our garden, not surprisingly, is strongly architectural in design – and perhaps that is right anyway within a walled garden.

Cleverly – and not of our contriving – it all starts out in the Mall, for to reach the garden you must walk in off the pavement up a paved path between cobbled areas and step down into a paved forecourt, through a gate in a fine screen of wrought-iron railings. Already you should be impressed by the pleasures of the house, with its many times indented front façades of warm brick, white-painted sash windows and columned porch. Come in through the double front doors and you will see you are on an axis through a narrow hall and up and out by a glazed door to the garden. Open that door and the axis stretches away up a long paved path.

That entry 'works' for everybody – it draws you in from light and space out in the Mall, through shade in the house into the privacy, delights and contrasts of the garden. It works the more because the path is tapered imperceptibly to increase the perspective, and ends with a white-painted seat against a dark background. More tricks are added, for there are steps up just outside the house to lawns surrounded by low retaining walls and steps up again to the main level. All this worked better still once, for there were three pairs of lead boxes on elegant stone pedestals, but the lead boxes were stolen.

The garden down by the house, being surrounded on three sides by retained beds and quite small, is intimate – its privacy made more secure by high walls, a spreading mulberry tree to one side and almost protected from the ever-present aeroplanes by the crown of a huge *Ailanthus altissima* and a thirty-foot *Eucalyptus*. It is a tranquil and confined space laid out with an oval of strong paving for sitting, almost an extension of the house itself.

The mulberry tree – there is a whole series of them in neighbouring gardens – must be about 150 years old. For as long as I can remember the tree has had its crown held together with criss-cross wires. Twenty years ago it shed a limb, which landed beside the pram with our youngest in it. The wires were promptly doubled and the children all survived! So ingeniously was the wiring done that it came as a shock to discover last year that the entire tree was leaning over one way more and more. Now the longest branches have been pruned back, the tree has been lightened and, suddenly, sunshine penetrates down to the grass below where it is badly needed – getting that grass to grow has always been a problem and almost as troublesome as disposing of fallen and fermenting fruit.

I came to live at Walpole in 1947. My grandparents bought it in 1926 and it was my grandmother, Mrs Robert Benson, who laid out much of the framework. To her must go credit, for it was most skilfully done. She had the retaining walls built around the lawns, then paved down by the house and planted the *Magnolia denudata* which now gives our sitting space shade. She was particularly proud of a double yellow tree peony, 'Souvenir de Maxime Cornu'. It grows here still, but ours is a much-travelled plant, for when she died my grandmother's plant was divided into bits for my uncles, a bit for Kew (where it still grows) and a bit was taken by her butler, Mr Ford. This because he was by then the gardener, having taken over for the war years when my grandmother's three gardeners retired or went into the Services. Mr Ford came back to help us in his retirement in the early 1950s, and later, when he emigrated to Canada at the age of seventy plus, he gave the peony back to Walpole.

Tree peonies are great favourites. I just wish they were not so difficult to establish – we now have fourteen, but must have planted forty. Undoubtedly the most free-flowering is a pink 'Moutan', which can produce sixty flowers, no trouble. It pleases me much that I grew it from a cutting. The most splendid is undoubtedly 'Superb'. That plant is now nearly twenty years old and it carries up to thirty huge cherry-red flowers. I know that I should prune it discreetly to promote base growth and bring the flowers down to a more comfortable level – but lack the courage.

Species peonies are also a favourite, and we seem to have one, grown from seed, *P. cambessedesii*, that makes our visitors plain jealous. It has early rich pink flowers, but its most enduring joy are the beetroot-coloured stems and the undersides to sage-green leaves. We grow others – yellow *P. mlokosewitchii, arietina, tenuifolia* etc. Their flowers are fleeting, but their foliage is good, and particularly so when young.

For me any garden of appreciable size must have wide lawns, not least because they create a sense of space and can link the various parts. Here they lead the eye through from one area to another. It would not do at all to be able to see everything from everywhere! But with five children the first purpose of the main lawn was for bicycling. Looking to the future, soon this will be dominated by a Tulip Tree, just given to us by our children and only nine feet tall but growing fast, and already colouring well in autumn.

Across the end of the lawn is a strict yew hedge – now grown to six feet high from personally sown seeds! Its purpose is to screen off and make secret secluded gardens beyond where *Cyclamen hederifolium* and all sorts of ground-covering plants grow well.

One more of my grandmother's contributions is the formal sunken lily pond laid out with retained beds all around. A pond with five children meant much worry, so

27. A combination of changing levels and tapered paving adds apparent length to the vista. The front door, the garden door and this main path are all on the same axis. The overhanging mulberry and *Ailanthus* trees provide shade and create contrasts of light.

28. The garden at Walpole House is a city garden of happy surprises not only for its sheer size and horticultural interest but also as an oasis of peace between a six-lane highway and the River Thames.

29. Seats are always welcome in a garden. Here in a hidden corner a seat affords a chance to admire the magnolias and contrasting foliage plants.

we fenced this garden off with secure gates and planted climbing roses on tight-stretched wires to make it impenetrable. A pot full of *Clematis alpina* 'Columbine' seedlings went in all around on walls and fencing and they are now most effective against the dark brick. But try to prune and tie in roses amongst delicate clematis growth and you will see that the mixture is not entirely to be recommended.

30. The white wrought-iron seat set against the dark yew hedge closes the vista from the garden door. *Pelargonium tomentosum* spills out over a magnificent vase.

Green flowers have great fascination for me – euphorbias and hellebores do well on our gravel and they would take over if the garden were neglected. Proudly we grow *E. mellifera*, a present from near Dublin, but sometimes a rare frost will cut it back. Varied and contrasting foliage also delights, none more than that of *Ferula communis* – brought back as a seedling from Sicily – with its countless golden flowers on stems up to fourteen feet tall. Alas, it only throws up such heads every two or three years, but with sun on the flowers against a dark background it is not to be missed.

Hidden up in the corner lies a little pool shaded by a huge *Paulownia tomentosa*, grown from seed, and chosen for its immense leaves, with ferns and rushes around the pool. By late summer this is all lush and green.

I have written of growing this and that from seed and indeed I find raising things from seed very satisfactory. Perhaps this is just economy – but how else can one come by great groups and some precious plants? Now that interest has led me on and we save seeds from many plants – reading a detective story for escapism is nothing compared to winnowing out chaff off a shaken tray into the fire all winter long! Now when the garden is open we almost give away thousands of little packets and I venture to think we have started off many young gardeners – a happy thought!

Inevitably the maintenance of two-thirds of an acre creates problems and some corners cannot be cut. The mower does much, indeed all the paths are set flush with the lawns and every internal corner has its 'mowing' stone. There is no time to plant out much, so almost everything has to be

31. The formal lily pond made by Mrs Robert Benson, Jeremy's grandmother, is a focal point. The grey stone of the paving slabs is relieved by clay pots tightly filled with hardy succulents.

achieved with permanent planting. Spring and early summer are the best time here, for it is difficult to sustain freshness on dry soil into the autumn. In winter we try to get everything clean and tidy, as in spring it is dangerous to move around on the beds until the buds are through. But even this is eased by setting foot-sized stones a pace apart on some beds, so that rain does not stop us and the soil is not packed down by careless treading – and the plants soon conceal the stones. From mid-April it is a race against time to get all straight for garden opening day. For me the housekeeping has to be perfect, even if the plants are not, and bare soil can be made to look good if well turned and picked clean of rubbish. That all this is possible says much

for Ursula Billington, who brought us up to standard over many years. Though she has now retired we still depend on her to supplement our other help. Even so, just before open days the family turns out and to them our thanks are due. Without them we would find it difficult to cope.

But it is just after the garden has been open that we enjoy the most. There is time then to sit still and enjoy it all.

39

Cottage Farm, Little Blakenham, Suffolk

Viscount Blakenham's Garden

We bought Cottage Farm in July 1945, in the middle of the General Election campaign. The house nestles under a ridge on a hill planted chiefly with beech trees. The view was exceptionally pleasing and we were situated bang in the middle of what was to be my constituency for eighteen years. The garden was pretty well non-existent. There was a small lawn by the front door, then a large croquet lawn stretching down to a spinney, the final feature being an attractive curved wall in which various alpines were grown.

We moved in in 1946. Our first task was to tackle the spinney, which was choked with elders and brambles. Even so, some eight years later about thirty trees, mostly larch and sycamore, had to be removed in order to let in more light. Fortunately for us Frank Knight was running Notcutts, our local nursery. He gave us a great deal of useful advice on what we could or could not grow on our strictly alkaline soil and helped us a lot with our original planting. Later he became Director of Wisley for a number of years. In the next two or three years we fenced in part of the meadow adjacent to the spinney, and constructed a swimming pool and tennis court hedged and fenced around with two large shrubberies of contrasting foliage plants.

Meanwhile we had thrown into the garden a small adjacent paddock, which had been used for the children's ponies. Along the road at the end of this new ground we planted a *Rosa xanthina* 'Canary Bird' hedge more than 120 yards long and a few specimen trees: *Aesculus indica, Fagus sylvatica* 'Riversii', *Magnolia soulangiana* 'Lennei' and *Liriodendron tulipifera*. All of these after more than thirty years make a fine show.

Meanwhile we were constantly gazing at Naboth's Vineyard. This was a five-acre wood, in the centre of which some fine trees had been cut down during the last war. In early May the whole wood was a sheet of bluebells, even coming out into our paddock, now part of the garden. We longed to be able to get this wood and create a magic garden within our own garden.

By a great stroke of luck the local farmer gave up his tenancy and I was able to buy both the farm and the wood.

We very soon decided that this new woodland garden could only be cleared in stages. It was essential however to agree the layout of the paths. These paths at the time of completion had hardly been altered from the original diagram and have pleased me very much. The shaping of the paths became a special task for my wife at which she has become quite expert.

So in 1951 the work of clearance started, which took eight years to complete. In charge was my loyal and talented head gardener, Mr Walton Barton, still with me after thirty years – semi-retired but taking a keen and constructive interest in all that goes on around him. He was assisted by George Calver, then aged fifteen. Some thirty years later he is the mainstay of our garden today. George Calver in turn is fortunate to have the help of an excellent young man, David Hardwick, who has been with us for eight years.

The wartime felling had been neatly done. Only high-quality oaks had been taken and a very adequate shelter belt had been left all around the wood. Brambles, nettles, elders and every sort of weed had to be cleared before planting could begin. Where possible we saved clumps of hazel and elder on which we planned to plant roses such as *R. longicuspis*, 'Wedding Day', *R. filipes* 'Kiftsgate' and 'Bobbie James'. This idea has worked out well. These clumps of roses, looking like massive bushes, make an attractive feature throughout the woodland scene. The new growth is entwined round each year and the bush gets slowly bigger and bigger.

A piece of real luck came our way. We soon discovered

that part of the wood had acid soil – apparently a pocket of green sand in the chalk. This was obviously going to give us a far wider choice of plants to grow. But with a rainfall the lowest in the United Kingdom (about eighteen inches) we realized that although rhododendrons might like our soil they would not appreciate the lack of rain. Although we had laid water on throughout the garden, it is pumped up straight from the artesian layer and has an extremely high chalk content, almost fatal to most acid-soil-loving plants.

Very soon it occurred to us that nothing would come of our planting unless we dealt with the rabbit problem. The whole of the garden, including of course the wood, was fenced and wired in. This has worked well and in recent years because of myxomatosis there have been no rabbits, but how long will this last?

By 1957 the clearing was over and the initial planting finished. Jim Russell, then with Sunningdale Nurseries, was good enough to guide us on the varieties and positioning of azaleas and rhododendrons. It was no easy task, but we very much like the colour combination of the various rhododendrons with the bluebells. In addition, acers, *Pieris*, magnolias, *Prunus*, *Malus*, and a large variety of species roses had all started and seemed happy in their new home. Thanks to the clearing the bluebells became even more splendid and remain so today. The soil was first-class and had benefited from at least 200 years of leaf mould from the removed oaks.

The grass paths, quite numerous now, are all self-sown – we ourselves have never put down one seed of grass. Although we have planted a large number and variety of plants we have always endeavoured to retain the wildness of the character of this wood and to prevent an impression of artificiality, never an easy balance to maintain.

32. A very fine example of *Wisteria sinensis* 'Alba' in a sheltered woodland walk.

33. A sinuous path traces its way through the wood, where bluebells succeed the daffodils.

34. The Cottage Farm garden is noted for its fine specimen trees and shrubs. *Cornus* 'Eddie's White Wonder' glows in a woodland setting.

35. In June *Genista tenera* 'Golden Shower' (until recently known as *G. cinerea*) provides a blaze of colour.

Birds continue to flock to us during the nesting period. They find us quite a sanctuary, because of the peace and quiet.

I would like now to mention certain features which I look forward to enjoying each year. *Magnolia campbellii*, planted in 1956, flowered first in 1978, then each year since. The plant in flower with its large cups of a deep mauve pink has to be seen to be believed. Next is a very showy plant indeed, *Cornus* 'Eddie's White Wonder'. My plant is a bush about twelve feet by twelve. It starts with lime-green bracts, which in a week or two turn pure white with a chocolate centre. It makes a really beautiful show. Both the *Cornus* and the magnolia were given to me by Sir George Taylor, late of Kew, whose kindness and generosity I shall always remember.

We planted a forsythia hedge, about seventy-five yards long, from the road curving up towards the house, which needs to be carefully watched, for unless it is sprayed at the right time the birds get all the buds: but we generally win. Around the house and on the other side of the road in front we have planted a lot of daffodils, a good mixture of early- and late-flowering ones. They came a sackful per year from the Scilly Islands, naturalizing well and flowering for a long period.

Once the bluebells and rhododendrons have finished the species roses take over. I have mentioned earlier how we have grown some of these as massive bushes round elder stumps. Some of my favourites are *RR*. 'Cantabrigiensis', *moyesii* 'Geranium', *webbiana*, *californica* 'Plena' and 'Mutabilis'. 'Cerise Bouquet', 'Constance Spry' and 'Lavender Lassie' are each well worth a place near to their more ancient brethren. Then in July the golden *Catalpa bignonioides* 'Aurea', which I planted more than twenty years ago and is becoming quite a large specimen, provides an excellent foliage colour contrast and looks beautiful against a large clump of the white *Rosa* 'Kiftsgate'.

From mid-July onwards the maintenance of colour in the garden becomes a problem. In the wood we have tried to solve this by planting a number of varying foliage trees – chiefly acers – *AA*. 'Crimson King', 'Drummondii', *negundo* 'Variegatum', 'Prinz Handjery' and *cappadocicum* 'Aureum' amongst others.

We have added quite a number of hydrangeas to give colour till the first frosts. In the wood *Hydrangea sargentiana*, *H. aspera villosa* and *H. heteromalla* seem happy, and there are clumps of *HH*. 'Blue Wave', 'Blue Boy', *paniculata* 'Grandiflora' and 'Lanarth White'.

I end with a brief word on autumn colour. Most of the acers colour well, as do the *Parrotia persica*, *Cotinus coggygria* and *Photinia villosa*. We have now established a *Nyssa sylvatica* and a *Liquidambar styraciflua* 'Aurea'. So throughout the garden there is usually some point where colour can be found.

So many kind friends have given me plants. Gardeners are the most generous breed of men. These presents form a sort of picture gallery reminding me of the donor and at the same time the circumstances during which the gift was made. Anyhow my garden has been greatly enriched by those kind people.

I am afraid that one of my great weaknesses is the love I have for this garden. There are golf bores, political bores and many other types of bores. I most certainly am a garden bore. The garden continues to fascinate me, and there is still plenty to do.

Blakenham

36. The 'Kiftsgate' rose provides a marvellous display. In July the golden *Catalpa bignonioides* 'Aurea' contributes an excellent foliage colour effect.

37. An astonishing display of *Rosa xanthina* 'Canary Bird', 120 yards long, lines the road adjacent to the paddock.

Stone Cottage, Hambleton, Rutland

John Codrington's Garden

This garden is about an acre in extent, on heavy, limy soil on the top of a hill facing north and east, in the former county of Rutland. Winds come unimpeded from Russia across the flat plains of northern Europe and over the North Sea.

My sister bought the place in 1951 and employed me to redesign the garden. She died in the early 1960s and left it to me in her will.

The first essential was shelter, for there were no trees except for a few apples near the house. Leyland Cypresses had not then swum into my ken so I risked *Cupressus macrocarpa*; this was successful, for they survived the terrible winter of 1962/3. I mixed in Lawson Cypress and Scots and Austrian Pines and later some of the grandchildren of *Cupressus sempervirens*, whose seed I had brought from the Garden of Gethsemane in 1925. And, of course, I also planted quick-growing deciduous trees – poplars, willows etc. I made a wood – about twenty yards by thirty on the north side of the garden – consisting of fast-growing common trees planted close together, and covered the ground with bluebells, anemones, cyclamen, hellebores, woodruff and Martagon Lilies. My sister complained of a lack of view, but I pointed out that it was a question of view plus north wind, or no north wind and no view and we agreed on the latter alternative. But now that Rutland Water has been created, I have put a seat in the wood and cut a gap (the Germans would call it an '*Ausblick*') which gives a magnificent view across an arm of this splendid lake to the opposite hill which could not have been better contrived by 'Capability' Brown himself!

Then the original plan had to be altered, for seldom had I seen such a dull country garden. It had a rectangular strip of lawn with a dreary, narrow border on each side, just like so many boring London gardens. There was an awful rockery-mound to one side. The only asset, and an important

one, was an old farm pond at the end of the garden. This is roughly oval, and about twenty yards by eighteen. It now houses a couple of ducks, called Simon and Judith, which were given to me as a present for my eightieth birthday, on St Simon and St Jude's Day. Simon and Judith have certainly cleaned the pond of duckweed, but they have also demolished my water-lilies and certain other treasures and are rather a mixed blessing!

I made a wedge-shaped incursion into the lawn filled with shrubs made for 'mystery' – one cannot now see what happens the other side until you walk round it. Opposite to the wedge are two bulges of mainly shrub roses, underplanted with scillas and *Viola cornuta*. On one side there is a plantation of green flowers and contrasting leaves – hellebores, euphorbias, *Ornithogalum pyrenaicum*, *Galtonia princeps* and green *Nicotiana* – and on the other, glowing against a dark evergreen background, a strident splash of orange and scarlet (roses, *Crocosmia*, *Lilium bulbiferum croceum*, *Lychnis*, *Cheiranthus* etc.).

The rockery was removed and a view was cut through and down to the pond: there is a cross vista in the middle, punctuated by four 'Sky Rocket' junipers.

Though I am generally not one for trying to grow calcifuges on an alkaline soil, I have succumbed to the temptation with a small area which was part of an orchard, some ten yards by eighteen, where I put down a 'couche' of peat and dug a few holes and filled them with leaf-mould etc. That was over twenty years ago and I have not renewed the soil. Yet the rhododendrons and azaleas I planted seem thriving, especially *R*. 'Praecox'.

My only sheltered and sunny border is under the house facing south, and here is my prize exhibit: I think I can boast that I have got the most northerly olive tree growing out of doors in England and therefore, probably, in Europe! I

38. A mysterious pool created from the old farm pond and surrounded by woodland and foliage plants such as *Euphorbia*, *Cyclamen* and hellebores. Weed-filled ponds obscure reflections, but here the water is kept clear by two resident ducks.

brought it from Malta about ten years ago; it very nearly died in 1978 but has recovered. Here also is a myrtle and just round the corner is an *Eriobotyra* (Loquat) which I brought as a seedling from South Carolina. Nerines, *Agapanthus* and *Zauschneria* are also happy here.

The pond area – indeed most of the garden – is very wild, for I am an amateur botanist and encourage wild flowers, which most people call weeds. Round the pond are masses of *Carex pendula*, Kingcups, Greater Spearwort (*Ranunculus lingua*), Meadow-sweet, Purple and Yellow Loosestrife, and the pale version of the wild yellow flag-iris.

Cow Parsley abounds everywhere – to the disgust of some of my visitors! – while the rather rare small teasels (*Dipsacus*

pilosus) as well as the ordinary ones sow themselves about the place, and so do mulleins and foxgloves.

Part of the much too large gravel drive I have let become a 'gravel garden'. Here *Briza maxima* has decided to take over and, to a lesser extent, the native *Briza media*. And here I allow Corn Cockle (*Agrostemma githago*) to seed itself. It is now probably extinct in the wild, as is also the pretty *Bupleurum falcatum*, whose seed I collected when it was fairly plentiful near Ongar, in Essex. This now seeds itself in the gravel very happily. Also here is the starry clover which once grew at Shoreham (my seed was from the Mediterranean). The Haresfoot Clover and the Hare's Tail grass also find homes here, and sometimes I can get the rare biennial

Campanula patula to seed, which grows in such pretty abundance in Austria and other places in Central Europe. Here, too, is the lovely sweet-smelling white mignonette which used to grow near Bicester. To give height to the gravel garden I have got some *Pinus densiflora*, which I grew from seed collected in the Imperial Park at Tokyo.

There is a 'Blue and Pale Yellow Garden' whose name describes it, and beyond this is a little enclosed white, grey and silver garden. It also includes touches of black, or almost black, tulips, *Geranium phaeum* and *Ophiopogon*. This garden has a *Yucca* I salvaged from a rubbish dump at the Generalife garden at Granada, as well as a fountain and a controversial 'focal point' in the shape of a Victorian stove in mock bamboo, painted white, which *I* like but some people don't!

As we are on to black and white, in front of the house among the roses I have a mixture of white and black tulips. I tried 'apartheid', separating the white from the black, and it looked all wrong. I have now got 'complete integration' and it looks lovely. Is there a lesson here?

I have an 'Orangery', originally a cowshed, but given a Georgian 'face-lift' with columns made from drainpipes. It holds some rather unhappy orange and lemon trees, amongst other not absolutely hardy things. I also have a small (thirteen feet by nine) tropical house which houses mainly so-called 'economic' plants – about the most extravagant and un-

40. A stone path is lined by an almost formal planting, with tiers of saxifrage, bluebells, the dwarf Purple-leaved Plum, backed with tulips, deep red honesty and dark green yews.

41. John, always original, has allowed part of the gravel drive to become a home for self-sown plants as well as carefully tended treasures which enjoy such conditions.

42. White flowers, golden variegated and grey foliage surround a pond where grows the sweet-smelling white-flowered *Apogoneton distachyos*.

43. Every inch of ground is covered. In front of a wall spilling with ivy and backed by the Golden Elder, grey grasses and ajugas multiply.

economic project I have undertaken! Here I grow the things one buys in the supermarket, such as cinnamon, coffee, sugar, sago, allspice, pepper, vanilla etc., as well as rubber, cotton, guava and castor-oil. The herb garden, about eight yards square, is near the kitchen; it contains about forty herbs, not all culinary, and is planned on a chequer-board pattern, with artificial stone slabs alternating with the herbs to stop them trespassing. Here also is an 'Agatha Christie' row of eight poisons, starting with a bird-sown plant of Deadly Nightshade (*Atropa belladonna*).

Finally, wherever I can, I have rough grass to make a good contrast in texture to the close-mown lawn. In it are naturalized not only the usual narcissi but also fritillaries, *Leucojum aestivum*, camassias, doronicums, wild geraniums, campions, ox-eye daisies, scabious and bedstraw, while *Smyrnium perfoliatum* and white *Geranium robertianum* seed themselves everywhere and are welcome.

Mine is a wild garden indeed and I like it like that!

John Codrington

44. St Fiacre, the patron saint of gardeners, entices the viewer to explore a narrowing brick and gravel path.

Abbots Ripton Hall, Cambridgeshire

Lord De Ramsey's Garden

A long time ago I was walking round the garden after breakfast with Lord Dacre of Glanton, now Master of Peterhouse, Cambridge, and better known as Hugh Trevor-Roper. I remember saying, 'I don't understand how even that modest squire's house came out of this heavy, poorly drained, cold, clay land.' 'It almost certainly didn't,' he replied and for the next hour fascinated me by a dissertation on the origin of wealth of English families. Since then I have learnt that good, chalky boulder clay, though rather too affectionate, is immensely fertile if well-treated and its idiosyncrasies respected, one of which is 'thorough' under-drainage in plastic pipes and, if necessary, automatically pumped, as some of mine has to be.

It grows huge elms and London Plane trees and a surprisingly large old ash for a heavy soil, as well as the very ancient *Magnolia grandiflora* that broke away from the south-west wall long before I came here fifty years ago.

I once told the late Sir Frederick Bawden: 'My head gardener says, what a pity there aren't more specimen trees.' He snorted, 'What's a specimen tree? Why, any well-grown one; it doesn't have to be rare, endemic or exotic.' Incidentally, he invented that ghastly word 'cultivar' and, not liking it himself, tried to recapture it, but it was too late. It escaped. Since then we have planted some of those so-called specimen trees: *Magnolia delavayi*, which shot up in fifteen years to the cornice round the roof. We started a collection of willows which, like roses, suit the land. I have planted forty or fifty species or cultivars in the garden which are grouped down by the river facing west. They are pruned back each year at three or four feet for the young growth. When there is an evening sun in winter I like going down to the opposite bank to enjoy the mixture of yellow, red and downy white colours.

Talking of the river in front of the house, rather than 'the drain', as my wife unkindly calls it, it runs round the Big Lawn, past the 'mounds' planted up with things like *Sambucus nigra laciniata*, past the gothic bridge, on under a brick bridge with the date 1746. Then it crawls through three villages, on and under the Great Whyte in Ramsey where the barges came up and finally into the Fen.

A large bank, twenty to thirty feet high and over a quarter of a mile long, was made by the road to deaden the noise of traffic and planted up by Lanning Roper. The west front of the house, overlooking the river, was rather dull, but brightened up by Peter Foster's 'treillage' and only lightly covered by *Trachelospermum jasminoides* in order not to spoil the false perspectives. Across the river is a fourteen-foot-high yew hedge with two groups of *Betula jacquemontii*. The hedge, dating from the eighteenth century, used to be continuous for about 130 feet. I am told that it hid what were then thought to be the indecencies of a kitchen garden. A charming family, long remembered in the village, rented the house in the 1890s. The then head gardener's daughter told us that Mr Gilliat wanted to cut a vista through the middle of it, but his wife disagreed. However, she went away for a few days and the deed was done.

Times were more affluent and the Gilliats moved the kitchen garden nearly 400 feet and made a double herbaceous border, backed with alternate twelve feet columnar yews and low golden *Philadelphus* bushes. The latter are too much in the full sun to stay golden long. The border runs through the gothic folly up towards the main road where it is joined by a red chestnut avenue.

I suppose, like us, the border is gradually becoming a museum piece. It is planted mainly to take over from the roses in July until the autumn, when the acers, *A. cappadocicum* 'Aureum' and 'Rubrum', *Sorbus* 'Joseph Rock', and *Malus tschonoskii* are even more spectacular than in spring.

I must now push on beyond the medieval mound, which Bacon would have commended, to the Edwardian rose pergola, which, in turn, leads to one of the vines (for colour, not for grapes) and the unique Jim Russell tropical house; turning back again through the rose pergola to the creeper-covered old brick wall and the all-the-year-round grey border. Then down past the fish pond behind the hedge to the grotto and over the river, through the Roman baths with their olives to the fern house.

For years, scarcely qualifying as more than garden boys, we have had much needed encouragement from real gardeners, one of whom told us this anecdote about a neighbour:

'I'm afraid I must give in my notice, Sir,' said the much-valued head gardener to his boss.

'Oh dear, oh dear, what can have happened?'

'Well, Sir, I have been very rude to her Ladyship. I called her an interfering old bitch.'

Mr X replied, 'Oh, you don't want to bother about that.'

We have to thank the retired head gardener from S—— nearby for much more than this charming story. Having risen through the ranks to the top he has given us the benefit of his vast practical experience from time to time.

One day two great gardeners stared at a large *Cotoneaster frigidus* and that lovely, yellow-berried *C.* 'Rothschildianus'. They turned towards each other and shook their heads – 'Fire blight, I'm afraid' (a notifiable disease), 'pull them up and burn them.' I was going to the Royal Horticultural Society that evening, so added a small sample to the few baubles I sometimes carry on these occasions. When I saw my man I asked for a favour – 'Of course,' he said. The answer came back promptly, confirmed by Cambridge labs – 'canker'. Never was a man more pleased to suffer from canker, now fully under control.

Walking towards the river we pause at the memorial urn on the plinth of which is a carved inscription 'Remember Humphrey Waterfield who made this garden anew'. A painter and dedicated gardener, always rather vague, on returning from France he sadly drove off on the right-hand side of the road.

45. The gothic folly designed by Peter Foster in painted iroko wood allows the garden visitor to pause a while on the long herbaceous border.

46. These herbaceous borders are magnificent from July to October, when the trees assume their autumn colour.

On, down amongst the old-fashioned roses which we love and which love us, mostly nineteenth-century French, we thank the Empress Josephine and Redouté but there are virtually none at Malmaison now. I don't think or thank often enough for all the things given us; those four variegated *Philadelphus* from Tony Venison, and a collection of hypericums from Allen Paterson of the Chelsea Physic garden, as well as other plants and seeds.

'Once bitten,' as Sir Alec Home said of fishing, 'fortunately you never recover.' Gardening is now our life, though sadly we realize that you can only garden for your lifetime. But how better could you spend your life?

47. The view from the house across the river. The main axis of the long border cuts through the eighteenth-century yew hedge.

48. Looking through the iris border over the Chinese Chippendale bridge. The *trompe l'œil* treillage gives winter protection to tender plants.

49. From the secret garden you can walk under the Edwardian rose arches to the grey and silver border.

50. Looking back towards the rose arches the grey foliage, red brick and lichened stone make a happy composition, packed with ideas for anyone seeking inspiration.

Hinton Ampner House, Hampshire

Ralph Dutton's Garden

For many centuries church and manor house have stood in neighbourly juxtaposition at Hinton Ampner on the summit of a long ridge which drops suddenly to the valley in which rises the River Itchen. In 1793 the existing Tudor house was demolished, and a trim Georgian building was erected which forms the central part of the present house.

The site is attractive with a wide southward view over undulating and well-wooded country without a building in sight. Thus the assets of the garden lie in the aspect and the prospect, combined with many mature trees. The drawbacks are the soil and the wind. The former consists of a layer of stony earth over solid chalk with an occasional pocket of heavy clay. Only on the north side of the garden is there a small area of deep loam.

The Georgian house seems to have had no garden beyond the walled kitchen garden. When in 1867 my grandfather altered the structure into a Tudoresque monster several grass terraces were formed. One improvement made by my parents was to unite these into a single broad unit and to bound it by a stone balustrade, intended to accord with the dubious architecture of the house.

In 1934 my father with some reluctance allowed me to make alterations below the balustrade, and I planned a sunk garden surrounded by a low wall with formal beds protected from the wind. In addition I made a wide grass path extending from one side of the garden to the other and passing in mid-course through the sunk garden. Along the western section I planted an avenue of Irish Yews, while the eastern section passed down a gentle incline to a grove of trees in front of which I later erected a statue of Diana. In these alterations I had the invaluable help of an enthusiastic young head gardener who, alas, died only a few years later. I have always been grateful to him for stimulating in me an interest in gardening which has never since waned. Having

inherited Hinton in 1935 on the death of my father, I soon began alterations to the house. A return to Georgian symmetry provided a central point from which the layout could radiate. The clumsy balustrade was a problem, but by widening the central steps, adding several bays at the west end and by lengthening the sunk garden, it fell fairly successfully into place.

On the east side of the garden was an old chalk-pit, which had, as Mr Brown would have said, 'capabilities'. For many years it had been used as a rubbish dump and was later abandoned to sycamore and ash seedlings, nettles and every sort of weed. All this was cleared away and the bare bones of the little dell were revealed, and very bare indeed it looked.

However, round the top perimeter we planted yews and other bushes to give apparent height to the sides, but suitable furnishing for the lower slopes was more difficult. As it happened I had lately read about Sir Frederick Stern's chalk garden at Highdown, behind Worthing, and finding a day when it was open to the public I visited it. There I found numerous fine plants, luxuriant hebes, brilliant peonies and so forth. I made notes, and plants were ordered and duly installed on the lower slopes of my dell during the winter of 1938/9. I felt confident that in this sheltered enclosure they would flourish, and I awaited the spring with happy anticipation. But, alas, disappointment was in store. By the middle of May it was abundantly clear that almost all my precious plants were dead.

At that time I was young in gardening, although not particularly in years, and it had not occurred to me that the garden at Highdown and my little dell resembled each other in only one particular – the soil. The former, as its name suggests, is sited high on a south-facing down where the salty air is seldom still, so frost must be negligible. Mine is a frost pocket *par excellence* into which the freezing air flows

51. A long grass walk passes through the sunk garden and on this western section is flanked by an avenue of golden and Irish Yews.

down and remains static, undisturbed by breezes. I had learnt a chastening but useful lesson. In the event this mortality mattered very little, for a few months later war broke out and the dell was once again abandoned to that rough gardener – Mother Nature.

At last the sad years of war ended, and in July 1945 I was back in my house gazing out onto the chaos of what had once been a well-kept garden. The wide terrace had been given up to rough grass, trodden by the two hundred little feet of the children who had inhabited the house during the war. We had no machine to do the work, nor petrol had we possessed one, but I was lucky finding two elderly men expert in the use of the scythe. Thus during the long summer evenings they spent many hours rhythmically mowing the rough herbage – a Millet scene – till the terrace had once again some semblance of a lawn.

Reclaiming the rest of the garden was a slow process spread over several years. I constantly bore in mind the lines of Alexander Pope in his Epistle to Lord Burlington on the planting of parks:

> Let not each beauty everywhere be spied
> Where half the skill is decently to hide,
> He gains all points who pleasingly confounds,
> Surprises, varies, and conceals the bounds.

Here then were my basic principles, but I would not for a moment hold that I have achieved them. I have, however, endeavoured to form vistas and to carry the eye out into the countryside without the intervention of visible fences.

One June day in the fifties I was taken to see the garden at Sissinghurst, and was entranced by the beauty of the shrub roses. They would not flourish so exceedingly at Hinton, that I knew, but I had at least a suitable place for them on the long south-facing bank behind the Irish Yews in my long walk. I planted many varieties, and since the soil here is a pocket of heavy clay, they do rather well.

From the eastern section of the long walk I created an attractive vista by leading the eye down an avenue of ancient limes which runs southward across the park, ending in a stone obelisk. At the top by the side of the walk I built a classical temple of modest dimensions as suits the site.

The works included a second reclamation of the dell. On this occasion only tough plants such as viburnums, shrubby spiraeas, herbaceous *Polygonum*, potentillas and so forth were used. Against the evergreens near the perimeter I planted some of the rampant rambler roses: *RR. filipes* 'Kiftsgate', 'Bobbie James', 'Wedding Day' and others. Now at mid-summer the dark foliage of hollies and yews is covered with a foam of white blossom. This, with the majestic if rather sinister stems of giant hemlocks which rise amongst the shrubs, provides almost the appearance of a tropical forest.

Between the church and the walled garden is an orchard where grass paths divide the area into four sections which in spring are bright with crocuses, daffodils and other simple

52. A long stone-paved terrace overgrown with shrubs, including *Hydrangea* 'Mariesii', ends with views of the Hampshire countryside.

53. The piers of the formal gate leading to the kitchen garden are covered with white *Clematis montana*.

54. The classical temple built by Ralph Dutton looks down on the long walk above the dell. A large *Cotinus coggygria* makes a good show to the right of the temple.

flowers. The east-to-west path is aligned onto the tall iron gate into the walled garden, beyond which a paved path between espalier fruit trees leads to a stone urn. Along this path I planted phlox, but the result was disappointing, and finding that the situation worsened we concluded that eelworm must be rife in the soil.

Unwilling to be defeated, we changed the soil and put in new plants, but still without success, and we felt at last obliged to accord victory to the pests.

The south–north path I bordered with irises which, though less calamitous than the phlox, were not successful – the flowering stems were usually blown to the ground. I was baffled for a satisfactory solution. But one spring day when sitting in the Jardin du Roi in the park at Versailles, I noticed the low box hedges surrounding beds of shrubs. Here, I decided, was the solution to my problems. Several hundred little box bushes were planted along the paths with yew trees at salient points later to be clipped into obelisks. The result is neat and labour-saving, and looks well all the year round. A path must lead somewhere and at first the south–north path had no objective, so, some years before planting the box hedges, I carried the path beyond the confines of the orchard into a small grove of beech and *Acer platanoides* 'Schwedleri' which I had put in before the war as a shelter from the north wind.

55. The sunk garden, created in 1934, below the paved terrace.

I found on analysis that the soil was almost lime-free, so here was an opportunity to plant shrubs which would be hopeless in other parts of the garden. Tall bushes of broad-leaved hollies keep out the wind, and the spring seems to come early to this sheltered enclosure. Camellias flower bravely here and in the rather damp soil *Primula japonica* seeds freely and raises its crimson spikes wherever it finds a congenial spot, while the frail and, it must be owned, rather sparse blossoms of azaleas fill the air with their pungent scent. The display is not sensational, but I like it. ''Tis a poor thing but mine own.'

Ralph Dutton

12 Alexander Square, London SW3

Francis Egerton's Garden

My very small London garden consists on the street side of three raised beds running along a public pavement with a backcloth of a six-foot brick wall and the house – all facing south. The inner garden is surrounded by this wall on three sides, north, west and east, with the rear of the house forming the remaining side.

I also have a roof garden leading off the first-floor landing of my house, facing west, surrounded by a palisade of perspex for wind protection, and a very small lean-to greenhouse placed next to the steps which lead from the house to the garden.

When I first came to live here in 1947 there was no garden except a patch of sour soil interspersed with broken bottles and bric-a-brac. The outside beds did not exist. I started the outside garden by building brick walls to contain beds with the main purpose of preventing dogs and cats fouling the plants and I surrounded these with a protective fencing and miniature hurdles with this in mind.

The inner garden I formalized by building sustaining walls round three sides and I dug out the old soil and replaced it with rich loam. In the middle I made a fish pond four feet deep, surrounding it with York paving stones and box balls at the corners, and I placed a lead fountain in the form of a dolphin in the middle.

When I started I wished to create a colourful garden of my favourite plants with particular emphasis and preference for plants that smell, lilies and annuals such as *Nicotiana affinis*. I particularly like Bearded Iris and I made three beds of these outside, on the pavement.

As time went on however, I found my selection of plants after flowering left the garden devoid of interest, especially in winter, and so I slowly evolved a different scheme and began to take an interest in evergreens and the interplay of various foliages. I dug up all the irises contained in the outside beds and substituted more architectural plants such as large clumps of *Yucca gloriosa*, Jerusalem Sage, *Senecio* 'Sunshine', *Aralia elata* 'Variegata', *Euphorbia wulfenii* and *Viburnum davidii*, with clumps of *Agapanthus* 'Headbourne Worthy'. Some of these I have clipped to produce a cloud effect which to me gives a sense of comfort and cosiness to an otherwise rather regular bed. I think this was influenced by some of the Italian gardens that I had seen. On the walls I planted a pomegranate tree, white and red japonicas (now called *Chaenomeles*) and a rose 'Mermaid'. These have now become very large.

In the other two beds I have many grey-foliage plants such as *Artemisia* 'Powis Castle' and *A.* 'Lambrook Silver', *Salvia argentea*, *Helichrysum* interspersed with *Salvia officinalis* 'Purpurascens'. Behind these is planted a *Jasminum humile* 'Revolutum' which has now achieved a height of fifteen feet and each year has to be cut back ruthlessly. It has a lovely scent and attractive yellow flowers.

In the remaining bed I planted a *Magnolia* 'Goliath', which has grown into a large tree almost ten feet high and flowers splendidly every year. Behind this is a *Vitis coignetiae* for autumn colour and in front groups of *Geranium* 'Johnson's Blue' and *Artemisia arborescens* interspersed with *Berberis thunbergii atropurpurea*, with a large rose 'Magenta' growing behind. In order to complement the Georgian façade of the house, I placed two black pots containing standard bay trees on either side of the front door, three large Italian terracotta pots filled with *Agapanthus praecox* along the façade, and three larger copper (verde antico) washing tubs, one with scilla and the other two with myrtle and *Yucca filamentosa* respectively. The former I have clipped into a large ball. All of these have flourished, but as the beds face south, copious watering is needed in the summer and a good mulching of peat, bone meal and manure prevents the soil drying out.

56. Looking down on the fish pond in this tiny inner garden in London. The fountain is a lead dolphin and the plants here are chosen for lasting effect.

57. The outside pavement beds are raised on low brick walls. Three large Italian terracotta pots are filled with *Agapanthus*.

The inner garden has been planted with *Camellia japonica* in red and white shades mixed with *Hydrangea sargentiana*, *Paeonia lutea ludlowii*, *Magnolia grandiflora*, *Skimmia*, *Ceanothus impressus* 'Notcutts Variety', and underplanted with *Hosta sieboldiana*, *Bergenia* 'Ballawley', *Helleborus corsicus*, *H. orientalis* 'Nigra' and *Salvia officinalis* 'Purpurascens'.

My great difficulty now is finding adequate space to put smaller plants, as the shrubs have become so big and produce thereby much shade and dry conditions. I built a small lean-to greenhouse butting onto the back of the house, which I find most useful for wintering house plants and some of my more tender pot plants. On the reverse wall of the house I have built a teak *étagère* painted dark green which holds a collection of about twenty large pots containing my favourite lilies, 'Green Magic' and 'Black Magic', Olympic Hybrids, 'Limelight', 'Imperial Silver', 'African Queen' and others. I

find the tier system facilitates watering and the shorter lilies can be placed on the top tier and the larger ones below. This makes a more attractive ensemble. Most of these lilies prosper but do not last for more than a few seasons in spite of heavy mulching and feeding.

The roof garden is very small – not more than five feet square – and consists of a lead platform surrounded by a low retaining wall. Into this space I have placed four pyramid box trees in pots on each of the corners and in the middle I have four medium-sized Italian pots filled with helichrysums surrounding a larger pot containing heliotrope 'Marine' in summer and Black Parrot tulips in spring.

On looking back over a period of thirty-four years in this garden, I realize that I was over-ambitious and tried to grow too many plants without allowing them enough room to succeed, and that this has been accentuated by my natural

58. Architectural plants have been used to give year-round interest. Copper pots are planted with myrtles and yuccas and a pomegranate flourishes against the wall.

59. Leaves of *Hosta sieboldiana* contrast with fierce yucca foliage.

60. Green is the predominant colour in the inner garden. Texture and leaf shape are all important.

distaste for uprooting plants which, however unsuitable in their surroundings, have served me well. My garden therefore has become rather a jungle. It has however been a labour of love and of absorbing interest despite the setbacks and ravages caused by household pets and other predators.

For those living in the heart of London, I recommend the interest that the interplay of various and contrasting foliages can produce. They never bore one and they add a touch of mystery which I find all-important.

61. Looking across the pond through heads of blue *Agapanthus* to *Hydrangea sargentiana* in full flower.

Blundells, Broadwell, Gloucestershire

Joe Elliott's Garden

I am always envious of the sort of person who can look at a barren piece of ground where a garden is to be made and after five minutes' thought knows that a border has to go here, a group of conifers there, a grass path leading to a sunlit seat must fill that space, with a pergola leading to a mass of roses to be viewed from the main window. Our garden did not come about in that way. In fact it is a Topsy garden; it just growed.

When we came here soon after the war the patch consisted of a tiny two-up, two-down cottage (much enlarged over the years) and two acres of scruffy plum trees and old cabbage stalks, growing – or dying – on a beautifully friable, easily worked limy soil. The whole area sloped gently to the south. I am sure one of those eager planners could have worked wonders if given a free hand but my wife and I decided that was not the sort of garden we wanted. One of the troubles was that in very early childhood I had been infected with a virulent and unconquerable virus – a love of all those plants which shelter under the umbrella heading of 'Alpines'. So the first priority was to find a home for the already considerable collection of these plants that I had re-assembled since the end of the war. In the vague mental plans we had formed of what should go approximately where in our new garden, there seemed no place where a rock garden would fit in naturally. The alternative solution came easily to hand however when we realized we were the owners of a dilapidated pig-sty built of mellow, well-weathered Cotswold stone. This was quickly demolished and rebuilt as a rectangular raised island bed bisecting the lawn we had sown in front of the house. It was about twenty feet long, five feet wide and eighteen inches high, with a foot-wide bed around its perimeter to give extra planting space and to facilitate mowing. I must say it looked pretty stark when filled with the gritty soil most alpines like and it was unkindly named

'The Grave' by the family – a name which has stuck to this day. But a year's growth of plant life soon converted it into a marvellously gay and flowery grave which I would be more than happy to find myself lying under when my time is up.

Since those far-off days, five other raised beds of various sizes have been built where they seemed to fit into the general garden scheme – or lack of it – and have been filled with a variety of soil mixtures, either to suit particular plants or to satisfy some experimental whim. One was given a half-and-half mixture of moss peat and pea gravel – our local gravel washed and graded to about the size of a fairly robust garden pea. Many plants have enjoyed this curious diet, particularly our native Chalk Milkwort (*Polygala calcarea*). Though this plant grows wild in several nearby turfy places it has always behaved as a rather sulky invalid in the garden; but in the peat and gravel it made beautifully compact six-inch tumps of dark glossy leaves, flowered prodigiously and even self-sowed in a most satisfactory way.

Another experimental bed was filled to its full fifteen-inch depth with neat pea gravel – no soil, peat or other dietary encouragement except a light dose of bone meal before the initial planting. Into this arid medium went plants which mostly, but not exclusively, were inhabitants of stony alpine screes. A surprising number of plants seemed to think that this apparent desert was what they had been searching for all their lives. The charming little *Dianthus* 'Hidcote' made a close-packed, two-foot sward of silver-grey leaves and flowered more freely than usual; *Teucrium ackermannii* grew to the same size in a couple of years and smothered itself in its pinkish-lavender flowers, much to the delight of the local bee and butterfly population. The little pink and white Moroccan daisy, *Anacyclus depressus*, flowered and sowed itself. Two spiny hedgehog plants, *Erinacea anthyllis* and *Vella spinosa*, in lavender-blue and primrose-yellow respectively, seemed to find these conditions just as congenial as those in which I had seen them growing together half way up the sunny side of the Spanish Sierra Nevada. The most surprising thing about this bed however was the fact that during the traumatic summer of 1976, when we went for nearly fifteen weeks without rain, it was never watered and practically every plant survived. There were many losses in nearby beds of more rational soil which *did* get an occasional can of water. Just what the reason is for this quite astonishing survival rate, in such an apparently hostile environment, I have yet to discover, though several interesting theories have been put to me. All my raised beds, incidentally, are in full sun, away from trees or buildings.

Another favourite method of growing my alpines has been in old stone sinks and troughs. It could be said I suppose

62. An impressive display of *Cypripedium reginae* grows in a stone trough.

that these handsome old receptacles have been allowed to dominate the garden, for over the years I have accumulated more than thirty, which now stand about the garden and my nursery edging the wider paths, on paved areas or anywhere else they seem to fit in happily and appropriately. Each is made up as a small rock garden, with a few carefully chosen rocks, and they house an immense number of my favourite miniature plants. Making the essential drainage holes in their bases was sometimes a problem, but on the whole Cotswold stone, which most of them are made of, is a fairly soft material which can be drilled or chipped without too much trouble. These, like the raised beds, are all in full sun except for four which nestle against the north wall of the

house and give homes to the relatively few shade-loving alpines such as ramondas, some of the hardy cypripediums, a few primulas and that absurd little gnome-like plant *Calceolaria darwinii* which comes from the grey, windswept areas around the Straits of Magellan, where one imagines the sun seldom makes an appearance.

Luckily, for the ultimate good of our garden, my wife's tastes tend to veer towards the larger more flamboyant forms of plant life, so that between the intervals of housing my beloved alpines we had been planting a number of trees and shrubs for background and backbone. Silver Birch, Scots Pine, several different forms of Lawson Cypress, *Prunus* 'Tai Haku', *Prunus yedoensis* (which we have seldom seen in flower because of the bullfinches; it just casts a nice shade on the paved sit-outery), a militarily straight line of Lombardy Poplars on our boundary and a screening hedge of *Chamaecyparis lawsoniana argentea* 'Smith's Variety', a form I have not seen or heard of since I bought it but which has proved itself quite excellent, of palish green with just the extreme tips of each shoot lightly flecked with gold. One or two borders of mixed shrubs and herbaceous plants came into being and here and there as the years passed some interesting effects began to show. One of the happiest was an *Acer platanoides* 'Drummondii' planted between the house and a well-established Purple Beech; the contrast of the golden sunshine of the *Acer* against the sombre beech is quite spectacular. A *Corylus avellana* 'Contorta' planted in isolation in about 1950 has now grown into a fifteen-foot giant; in summer it is no more than a pleasant green blob, but the twisted and contorted bare stems against the winter sky are a constant fascination.

A host of modern Hybrid Tea and Floribunda roses fill a forty-yard bed, backed by mixed shrubs including *Ptelea trifoliata*, which I am always surprised not to meet more often in other gardens. Its pendant clusters of greenish-yellow flowers almost rival the roses in wafting their delicious scent on a warm June day. Of our older and species roses, the most rewarding has probably been *Rosa californica* 'Plena', planted in grass at the edge of the orchard. It is on its own roots and had it not been for the thrice yearly mowing of orchard grass it would probably have taken over the whole garden by now, for its suckers appear many yards from its original position. It is now eight feet high and has been allowed a spread of four or five yards. In early summer its gracefully arching stems strung with semi-double blooms of warm, rich pink make a fine show.

Our modest patch has evolved over the years into a collection of plants rather than a spectacular planned garden. But it has given us both tremendous enjoyment as just that. Perhaps subconsciously I have tried to emulate the advice given by that great man Professor Sir William Wright Smith

63. A formal line of troughs dominates the path beside the house, each one a miniature rock garden. They sustain interest throughout the year.

64. Tufa shapes are carefully positioned within troughs to resemble miniature landscapes.

65. A flaming *Phygelius capensis* contrasts with the grey foliage at its feet.

when he took the first lecture I attended as a young man at the Royal Botanic Gardens, Edinburgh. He told the group of new students that during the three-year course we were starting we should try to learn something of everything and everything of *one* thing. Heaven forbid that I should claim to know everything there is to know about alpine plants (one of the joys of gardening is surely that one never *does* stop learning) but it is very sound advice – and not only for gardeners.

Joe Elliott

66. Joe has collected more than thirty old stone troughs over the years to accommodate his collection of alpines.

67. The raised bed eighteen inches high nicknamed 'The Grave' is filled with gritty soil to suit a collection of alpines.

The Garden House, Buckland Monachorum, Devon

Lionel Fortescue's Garden

On my retirement in 1945 from Eton, where my wife and I had planted a garden of lime-tolerant plants, we decided to move to the West Country, with its favourable climate for gardens. Our choice was the Garden House, a name we gave it before getting to work on the neglected old walled garden on a steep north-facing slope below the house. The house is on a hillside to the west of Dartmoor, in a small valley running down to the River Tavy, sheltered from the south-west and north. The stony soil looked poor but, fascinated by the beauty of the landscape, I sent a soil sample to the Devon Agricultural College for analysis. The chemist kindly brought the analysis, looked at the site and said that with generous treatment it would grow a wide range of plants. What we did not know until later was that the soil in the lower half of the walled garden is alkaline, pH 7 to 8, the result of long cultivation, whereas above it is acid, as in the surrounding meadows, pH 5.5. This has enabled us to grow both lime-loving and ericaceous plants in close proximity to each other, a very effective combination.

One of our first tasks was to plant a windbreak against the north-west and north-east winds, for which we chose *Cupressocyparis leylandii*. A compromise had to be reached between the need for shelter and for keeping views of the valley and of the Cornish hills beyond. These trees were planted up and down the slope and not across it, so they do not impede air drainage. Today they not only provide shelter but also add almost a sculptural quality to the garden, in which hedges of numerous genera provide a recurring theme. The final fact that decided us to buy this place was that my wife went to look at a house and garden near Crediton (a few miles from Exeter), where a spring frost had just caused damage in the garden, whereas here there had been no frost.

In 1945 we bought with the house some four acres of land. This included the old walled garden, on the steep, north-facing slope immediately below the house. The upper part of this is terraced, with retaining walls in some places of great height, according to the lie of the land. There are altogether five levels, of which the two bottom ones are extensive and only partly terraced by low retaining walls. The enclosing wall is not stepped but runs in a smooth line approximately parallel to the ground.

A prominent feature is a large barn on the bottom level running from north to south, which projects beyond the boundary wall. As the roof was in a very bad state and had to be replaced we decided to thatch it. At one time there was a second storey, reached by a spiral staircase, the grey wall of which juts out into the garden. On the opposite side of the main grass path is an old tower with a spiral staircase. This was the entrance to the fine three-storeyed house built by the Abbot of Buckland Abbey at the time of the Dissolution of the Monasteries by Henry VIII. The Abbot changed his cloth and became a village priest. It was the King's policy to treat the abbots generously as compensation for the loss of the abbey revenues. Dr Hoskins, the well-known authority on Devon architecture, says that in fact parts of the tower are earlier than 1530. When the vicarage was moved up the hill to the site of the Garden House, the former vicarage was pulled down with the exception of two storeys of the entrance tower still standing.

The gardens and lawns in front of the house we made. We also planted the avenue of *Prunus* 'Tai Haku' and other trees and shrubs, which make the entrance drive so attractive.

To return to the walled garden. The trenching of the soil was unexpectedly laborious, owing to the large pieces of shillet that had to be removed. The local representative of

64

the Agricultural Service obtained for us at low cost four prisoners-of-war from a nearby camp. They were brought and fetched away by lorry. After a year they were repatriated and replaced by European voluntary workers. They all worked very well and our gardener was with them. So for two years five men were at work in the garden and in the lower part of the adjacent meadow. From both tons of stone were removed and blocked land-drains repaired.

The soil was enriched with bracken, peat and cow-dung. The acid soil (the top part of the garden) is planted mainly with *Pieris*, camellias, rhododendrons, deciduous azaleas and is mainly spring-flowering. There is also an enormous specimen of *Magnolia salicifolia*.

Below, in the limy soil, are some good forms of *Magnolia soulangiana*, including a beauty given to us by the Professor of Botany at Coimbra University in Portugal; it is hitherto unknown in this country. There are *Philadelphus*, deutzias and roses. There are also herbaceous borders of carefully selected plants. In August various eucryphias and hoherias are in flower.

This north-facing slope is an excellent site for a garden. The evergreens of the upper terraces and above them a very old *Rhododendron arboreum* and a Purple Beech provide a background. As one looks across the slope, the sun coming down through foliage and flowers shows them up to their best advantage.

Owing to the limited space available, the qualifying test for plants has to be severe. We search for the best forms and pay great attention to our grouping for colour, form and foliage.

The entrance is on the road down to Buckland Monachorum. On the right is an old yew tree, on the left a group of mahonias of our own raising, then some *Camellia × williamsii*; next, at the back, a line of *Rhododendron augustinii*, propagated from good forms we saw in private gardens, whose owners kindly gave us cuttings. In front, along the drive are unusually good forms of *R. williamsianum*, also from private gardens. Next, there is a young tree of the best form of *Magnolia sprengeri diva* and a group of young shrubs, including *Taxodium ascendens nutans*, close to the neighbouring house and a unique form of *Cornus nuttallii*, seen by Mr Hillier on a dendrological tour, of which we were members. He obtained propagating material from the owner and sent us a plant, labelled *Nuttallia* 'Portlemouth'. It had its first flower in 1980.

Rhododendrons and deciduous azaleas are the most difficult to place. Fortunately they can be transplanted when in flower and a plant beautiful in itself may be banished from our garden. Growth of plants here is extraordinarily rapid and after a few years the garden had the appearance of being well-established. The winter of 1979/80, with a freezing gale followed by frosts with temperatures falling to zero Fahrenheit, killed all *Ceanothus* and some other plants, badly damaging many others. However, the latter are already well on the way to recovery.

The peak of the flowering season on the acid soil is in May; on the alkaline soil it is from mid-June onwards but in the walled garden there is always some section in flower. As at Sissinghurst, the walled garden is divided into sections, but here it has the advantage of being terraced. The terraces

68. A garden created on five levels. There is a happy compromise between the need for shelter and for keeping views of the valley and the Cornish hills beyond.

69. The different sections of the walled garden provide vistas and surprises.

70. The crimson *Rhododendron arboreum* and various creamy-white crosses produced at the garden, including 'Katherine Fortescue'.

71. A successful May combination of *Meconopsis* and the deciduous *Azalea* 'Warrington'.

72. In the walled garden the soil is acid on the higher levels and alkaline on the lower levels, the result of long cultivation.

73. Overgrown ruins add a sense of age to this garden created by the late Lionel Fortescue in his retirement.

enable us to accommodate a large number of plants. For instance, immediately above the magnolias, at the base of a high retaining wall we have planted eucryphias and other shrubs. Our walled garden is considered one of the best in the country. The acreage of our land to the west has been increased by the purchase of four acres from the Church Commissioners. We handed over all our land to the Charity Commission some years ago, so it is now a charitable trust and safe from any building development.

On two afternoons a week, when plants are offered for sale, the gardens are open to the public in aid of the National Gardens Scheme.

The future of the garden seems assured after our time, as our young head gardener and his wife were both trained at Wye Horticultural College. He is a hard worker and very observant, and has good taste. He gets on well with our under-gardener, who has worked here for nearly forty years.

L. S. Fortescue

Marsh Lane, Harlow, Essex

Sir Frederick Gibberd's Garden

My garden is in a new town – Harlow. Strangers commiserate, but I designed the town. I also designed the garden and it too is new – the town is thirty-six and the garden twenty-six years old.

I bought the site, the side of a small river valley, in order to make a garden, a selfish, intense and absorbing pleasure. It was ideal. The setting is a beautiful almost self-contained stretch of Essex countryside. There was no garden to speak of, the house was a mock Tudor bungalow, and the farm buildings had no architectural pretensions. A fine avenue of limes, some old trees and a two-storey summerhouse were all that needed preservation.

The garden is roughly symmetrical about a north-to-south axis. The house, on high ground, is close to a cart track which forms the southern boundary. From there the site slopes down to a flat valley bottom where a small river forms the northern boundary. On either side water meadows stretch along the river. The soil is a heavy loam over a mixture of clay and flints, with pockets of sand on the high ground and a deep silt over clay in the valley bottom. Springs abound and the water table in the valley is just below the ground surface – I only have to dig a hole to have a pool.

'Consult the genius of the place.' Such variety in the topography gave me the opportunity to form areas of distinctive character (landscape vistas, terraces, woods, glades, pools, streams, bogs) and, being of the place rather than superimposed, they look natural.

Garden design is an art of space, like architecture and town design. The space, to be a recognizable design, must be contained and the plants and walls enclosing it then become part of the adjacent spaces. The garden has thus become a series of rooms each with its own character, from small intimate spaces to large enclosed prospects.

I started making the garden adjacent to the house, worked slowly down the valley to the river and then outwards on either side until it is now about six acres, larger if landscape vistas are included. But I could not wait to bulldoze a pool in a bend in the river and make a waterfall, so I planted trees in anticipation of future development – regrettably in dozens instead of scores.

I related the rooms or spaces to the character of the topography in which they occur; adjacent to the house they are geometric, down the valley slope they become less formal, until in the valley bottom everything becomes completely natural. There are sequences of spaces in all directions. A focal point in one area draws you on into the next. The design is a cellular one to be explored – quite different from a public garden where paths form a structure leading you from one delight to another.

While all the rooms have their own character they are not self-contained like a rock garden or a white garden. The plants that enclose a space contribute to those adjoining, and the spaces lead imperceptibly into each other – perhaps the most difficult design problem of all.

A work of art requires unity as well as variety. This arises from my feeling or intuition and respect for the existing character.

I work with nature, not against it, and use only plants that will thrive in my area. From trees to ground cover I try to devise compositions that will look after themselves. There are no annuals and no herbaceous borders, although I use common species like *Solidago* and *Aster acris* in big clumps to give blocks of colour in distant views and a fine haze in winter. Plants that require much care and attention like alpines are confined to small pockets in pavings – we only have the help of a handyman and boy.

I choose plants for their shape, texture and colour, or for their capacity to form dense screens (essential to an art of

74. An architect's garden spread over six acres. It progresses from the geometric near the house, as in this patio garden, to the informal where the garden stretches to the river.

75. Columns rescued from the demolition of Coutts Bank in the Strand make an outstanding feature in a garden packed with sculptural surprises.

76. From trees to ground cover to pavement planting, compositions are devised to look after themselves. The siting of the collection of both old and specially commissioned sculpture, perhaps the largest private one in Britain, is all-important to this garden.

concealment), and I grow lots of 'weeds'. Daisies painting a lawn white, or speedwell blue, are not, for me, plants in the wrong place.

A garden which collapses in winter can hardly be called a design and to sustain the character there are many plants that make good screens – privet and laurel, holly, yew or box back up decorative shrubs and in the valley bamboos form impenetrable screens. I avoid areas that collapse after the autumn and do not try to extend the flowering period.

If a particular species tends to become rampant I let it take over, removing its neighbours or if need be changing the

77. The avenue of limes, an already established feature when Sir Frederick began creating this garden, matches the grandeur of the rescued stone columns of the 'Roman' ruin.

line of a path. Plants, like the human species, are not always splendid specimens and I spend time pruning and trimming them into their characteristic shapes. The weaklings I eliminate, much to the distress of my wife.

Grass, our national ground cover, gives cohesion to the areas. From the house down to the river it assumes the form of the ground it covers and I grade it from lawns round the house to rough grass in the valley. Ease of grass cutting and my ideas on design coincide: there are no sharp bends or angles and no obstruction from small flower beds. Where I have them, these are in paving.

In my anxiety to form screens and cover the ground I plant far too closely, letting plants grow into each other instead of being surrounded by earth so that each can thrive and be seen to its best advantage. It is not a precise garden, but neither is there the profusion of the cottage garden.

After some years the house was rebuilt, which gave me the opportunity to relate the art of garden design to that of architecture. Walls were extended outwards to form patio gardens, and gardens were made for the three living-room windows – a vista over the valley, always changing, a restricted view into a small walled garden always green with camellias, rhododendrons and *Fatsia japonica*, and a conservatory vivid all the year with geraniums.

Objects from sites I have worked on find their way into the garden as incidents in the natural scene. Carvings from an Oxford college are built into a retaining wall, a font from a church in Leamington Spa is now a plant container, huge boulders from Llyn Celyn reservoir border a pool. Columns rescued from Coutts Bank in the Strand were an excuse for making a glade with the 'Roman' ruin (Harlow was a Roman settlement) as its focus.

My wife and I collect sculpture. She buys immense works by young sculptors and we have the fun of finding sites which enhance both them and the garden. Sometimes the right site does not exist and so a garden is made as a setting. Sometimes a particular view of the garden seems to demand a sculpture and failing to find the right work we commission one – a fascinating process, for the sculptor's eye is not always in sympathy with the garden designer's.

In my race against time I have the advantage of mechanical equipment. Recently I spent a week's holiday with the driver of an immense excavator. Together we dug a moat, formed a mound with the spoil, and surmounted it with an elm-log castle – a wild folly but also enjoyed by my grandchildren.

Fredk Gibberd.

78. Garden and house are linked by carefully calculated views from the living-room windows. Here the eye is led to a distant view over the valley.

79. The conservatory, vivid all the year with geraniums.

The Priory, Kemerton, Worcestershire

Peter Healing's Garden

The Priory may not have housed pilgrims who visited the abbeys of Tewkesbury, Pershore and Evesham, but many old tales linger on about the house and its immediate surroundings. At least it has a ruin, probably of the sixteenth century, and a great clipped yew tree some twenty feet high; but more important to us it has been our home for forty-five years.

The garden lies on the southern slopes of Bredon Hill, 250 feet above sea level, with views on a clear day to the Bristol Channel and the Welsh hills, a site believed to have been favoured by the Romans for their vineyards.

There are four acres under cultivation, bounded on either side by small swift-running streams, and until my wife started planting mulberries, walnuts and *Acer* in variety towards the end of the war the garden was greatly lacking in trees of any calibre or indeed features of any kind. The only guidelines were three herbaceous borders, two running north to south and the third below the ruin and close to the house.

From these bare bones the garden has developed and greatly changed, although help has been very much reduced. Small new sections seem constantly to be springing up and this has been made possible by changing methods and by denser planting.

By the end of the war I found myself in Germany with only one book, William Robinson's *English Flower Garden*, perhaps one of the best garden books ever written, and it was through him that I pictured the form that the borders must take. It was essential that they should have a well-defined plan if they were to avoid the haphazard appearance that so many seem to possess.

The main border, some 150 feet long and now eighteen feet wide, was planned to start with grey foliage through white, cream and pink to pale yellow, working up by strong yellows to a crescendo of reds, maroon and bronze. From there it would fade gradually in the reverse order down to whites and greys in the far distance.

The second border was to be whites and creams, with pale pinks and lavender, while the cross-border under the ruin would be every shade of red. It would never become garish or too strong as there are so many really dark reds and bronze flowers and foliage to choose from and these would absorb the heat of the scarlets.

Such ideas were translated into yards of planting plans and proudly transported home at the end of the war. Little was it realized that not only were very few of the plants or seed available but that these quantities would involve much propagation. Here lies, perhaps, one of the great pleasures of gardening which I hardly visualized at the time. Progress is always slow, sometimes imperceptible, until one day – maybe years later – the vision seems to become reality. And so it has been with the borders, and I am still finding plants from my original list. Only this year I discovered *Lobelia tupa*, praised and illustrated by Robinson, but almost lost to cultivation. This splendid acquisition is now in the border below the ruin and is joined in high summer by the many tones of red of the Willow Beet, with leaves like patent leather (an ornamental form of *Beta vulgaris*), 'Ruby Chard', and the tender iresines. The middle ground of this border is held by *Lobelia cardinalis* 'Dark Crusader' and *Dahlia* 'Bishop of Llandaff', mixed with *Ricinus gibsonii* and bronze-leaved cannas. Old red roses, penstemons, monardas backed by the purple-leaved nut and the darkest *Cotinus*, should make the border overflow like a cornucopia. Perhaps on summer evenings that almost comes true.

The framework gradually developed, greatly helped by planting a long yew hedge with buttresses on the south side, which formed a dark background for the long border.

72

80. A hidden 'June' garden has twin beds planted with soft colours and greys, backed by banks of old roses and tall shrubs. The centre path, over which the plants scramble, is made from the tops of staddle stones found in the garden.

81. A raised bed of alpines gives interest from spring through to the autumn. Flowering here are *Cistus* 'Silver Pink' and *Carpenteria californica*.

82. A special feature of this garden is the red border, with its clever combinations and juxtapositions, at its best from August onwards.

Behind this hedge there is now a garden designed to bridge the gap between spring and high summer, for it is in this latter period, from mid-July to the end of September, that the borders come into their own. No attempt is made to 'have a bit out all the time'.

This 'June' garden is of soft colours, starting with clumps of the common seakale, *Crambe maritima*, and the wild Eryingium of our seashores, the finely feathered *Artemisia arborescens* 'Faith Raven' and many other greys. Thence to the whites of *Malva moschata alba*, the species *Phlox paniculata* and *Campanula pyramidalis* (the Chimney Bellflower). There are many other campanulas and pinks which change from year to year as different forms are grown from that treasure, the Alpine Garden Society's seed list. The centre path, over which the plants scramble, is made from the tops of staddle stones found around the garden and the whole is enclosed into its own little world by high banks of old roses, particularly 'Ispahan' and 'Clair Matin', which grow so strongly on their own roots. Gaps are permanently filled with that old favourite viola in green and brown, 'Irish Molly'.

An early acquisition was three seeds of *Datura suaveolens*, of which one germinated. This and its many progeny have given endless summer pleasure, with great white lemon-scented trumpets. To this has been added a number of other varieties which are grown in large tubs in a small sheltered rose garden near the house. Robinson pictures them planted out in grass in the open, but their two enemies, high wind and red spider mite, are better contained with the protection of walls.

In the shade of these tall plants grows *Clematis florida* 'Sieboldii', like a small delicate passion flower and yet tough enough to stand the winters of twenty years.

To the south of this sheltered garden lies the border along the front of the house and a sunken garden carved from the ruins of an old wool-bleaching building. Here is a concentration of ferns, lilies and double primroses. The ferns are happy and the many varieties came as tiny plants from that doyen of the fern world, Reginald Kaye. The lilies find the heavy alkaline clay not entirely to their liking but strangely that great beauty, *Carpenteria californica*, grows larger every year.

Surrounding the sunken garden there are a number of raised beds where at waist height many alpines grow, and there is a collection of the old named *Primula marginata*.

The border in front of the house is planted in the main with tender subjects. One of the exceptions is the grey-leaved, dark-purple-flowered *Calceolaria arachnoidea*, a dusky favourite from Chile which seems to come through any

83. The pergola leads from the old ruin to the stream garden. The pillars are smothered with a selection of climbers including *Rosa* 'Albéric Barbier' and *Clematis viticella* 'Plena', and for autumn colour there is *Parthenocissus henryana*.

winter. Many salvias grow against the wall. In the front there are plants from the Canary Islands, *Lotus berthelotii* A.M. (which flowers with scarlet 'lobster claws' in the cool house), *Senecio heritieri* and hopefully *Echium wildpretii*. These are backed by a large *Abutilon vitifolium* and *Cassia corymbosa*.

From this part of the garden there is a short spring walk through shrubberies where hellebores and cyclamen are backed by the yellow *Ribes laurifolium*, so welcome in February.

There is always the hope of increasing the variety of interesting and rarer plants. Visitors kindly arrive with some, while others come from botanic gardens during our summer excursions, which are part of the endless joy to be found in the world of gardening.

Our gardener, Charles Brazier, who came to us over thirty summers ago, has watched the changes in the garden and indeed has made them possible. Without his unfailing help much of the garden would still be only on fading parchment rolls of hopes and dreams.

84. The lily-covered pool in the centre of the sunken garden carved from the ruins of an old wool-bleaching house. Ferns, lilies, double primroses and *Meconopsis* in variety flourish in this sheltered spot. Tubs of *Datura* stand out here in summer.

Saling Hall, Great Saling, Essex

Hugh Johnson's Garden

It is one of the paradoxes of making a garden that the more you pack into it, the bigger it gets. There are quite big gardens you can take in at a glance, and tiny ones that will absorb you all afternoon. How? Because they reveal themselves bit by bit. They are subdivided into separate compartments, each with its own mood. The change may be in scale, in colour, from simplicity to richness of detail, from an open sky to the shade of a tree; the important thing is that the mood changes. Each change rekindles the interest and makes you ready for more.

That, at any rate, is my philosophy in planning the garden at Saling. We live in bald, featureless farmland, stripped, since we came here ten years ago, of the scores of tall elms which were its hills. I sometimes think – probably deluding myself – that if we lived in beautiful country with meadow, wood and stream my gardening would stop at a rose over the door. But here one gardens in self-defence. I plant to make a fantasy world more sympathetic than the level acres of beet and beans all round. The first object of the garden is seclusion (which includes shelter from unfettered winds). Within that seclusion I look for variety of mood.

Thus the visitor, coming to the front gate, finds himself on what seems like (and once was) the village green. The duckpond with its willows lies in front of a little white farmhouse. A double row of Lombardy Poplars leads to the church gate. There is nothing more exotic than Horse Chestnuts and a clump of flowering cherries. This is the view we see from the front windows of the house.

Drawing nearer, the visitor passes a young Cedar of Lebanon and between two wings of yew hedge into a walled yard. There are roses on the flanking walls, vines on the house; only a slight quickening of the pace of horticulture.

So when he turns left through a door in the wall into a walled garden as trim as we can make it, where brightness of colour is combined with formality of plan, he has a distinct sense of having come straight to the heart of things. I have noticed in Kyoto how the Japanese hold everything in check, even make you pass through a little courtyard of total simplicity, like an airlock between different pressures, before showing you one of their perfect set-pieces. That is the effect I aim for.

After the formal, the obligatory, introduction the visitor has a choice of ways – a little labyrinth of yew-walled yards, of closely hemmed-in paths, of secluded corners, before the scale changes completely to open glades and scattered trees; then to a belt of young trees which in turn hides a long lawn stretching away between trees on gently rising ground each side to a pond with a rustic bridge a hundred yards away.

This is pure fantasy-land where anything goes. It bears no relation to the country round. The trees are a mad mixture of shapes and colours. I have tried to make scarlet tulips look like wild flowers. In the austere context of arable Essex, with only the odd neglected oak forlorn in the flat fields, the frivolity of it is pretty shocking. It needs screening deeply and thoroughly, both for its own sake and that of the honest-to-god countryside. When the elms died this meant a rush of planting willows, Leylands, Field Maple and hawthorn, ash and oak, to make a wall as fast and high as possible.

The pond and its bridge are a recent addition intended to draw the visitor on to investigate the far end of the garden. Somebody has likened good garden design to a golf-course, where each tee has a hole in sight, and each hole a tee to drive off to the next one. The bridge is the hole from the near side of the lawn, and the tee for investigating the newest feature of the place, still very much in my mind's eye; a formal beech walk to a seat.

From the seat you drive off again up a poplar avenue (the whole of this area was a poplar plantation until five years ago; to make an avenue I had only to leave two existing rows) to a large stone ball salvaged from the old Knightsbridge barracks. From there it is a wander through a little wood of oaks to a grassy hollow dominated by a particularly shapely spreading one.

Beyond the hollow is another little wood, this time of Norway Maples, and beyond that a grove of larches (all these making our eastern windbreak). But the visitor will probably choose to come back to the house down a grass alley between roses, peonies, lilacs and things, beckoned on by the stone balustrade of a flight of steps down to a water garden.

It all sounds very complicated – and it is. But what I am trying to stress is that the mood keeps changing. Here are openings; there dense trees of one species in sufficient number to feel like a wood. Here is a little shady pool; there an open sunny pond. For the cold east wind of spring there

85. (*above*) A flight of steps with stone balustrade leads romantically towards a water garden, planted with bold juxtapositions of shape and texture.

86. Among the many deliberate moods in this garden are that of melancholy and romance discovered in the static reflections of the water garden.

87 and 88. In winter the rectangular central beds in the walled garden are given form by a double line of Irish Junipers, pyramids of clipped box to emphasize the corners. Tall, clipped and sentinel-like, a row of *Chamaecyparis lawsoniana* 'Pottenii' gives an air of grandeur.

89. In summer the outline of this formal garden is dissolved in a riot of exuberant planting.

is a little thatched barn facing west towards cherries and pines; for blustery westerly days another little summerhouse faces east over the water garden.

This is my place for revelling in rain. We live in a parched part of England where rain is a positive pleasure. I learned from the Japanese the delight of watching and listening to rain in a garden from under a good dry roof. I watch it drip from Swamp Cypresses, rattle on *Gunnera* leaves, weigh down arching bamboos.

I must emphasize that all this is very young. We have twelve acres, and I have only been gardening here in earnest for nine years. During that time my intentions were radically altered by the death of the elms (we lost fifteen trees of more than twelve-feet girth, and scores of smaller ones).

With the elms gone, the dominant trees over most of the place were 'match-stick' poplars – very pretty in spring with russet leaves and in autumn with yellow, but terrible neighbours for younger plants. I tried living with them, and planting the trees I wanted under them, for three years before I realized that any benefit they gave as shelter was far outdone by their greed. The poplar roots instantly penetrate the holes prepared with good stuff for new plants. So far, therefore, we have cut down over five hundred poplars, and there are still more to go.

The last owner, Lady Carlyle, had been a keen and discriminating gardener in the fifties, and we owe her a great deal. Twenty-five years have been enough for many of her trees to become impressive characters: *Taxodium* and *Metasequoia, Ginkgo* and *Parrotia, Acer cappadocicum, Prunus* 'Ukon' and 'Shirofugen', *Robinia* 'Frisia', flowering crabs and Judas Trees. A pleached lime alley of hers is splendid in maturity. Several excellent shrubs survive – most notably a huge *Abelia triflora* that weeps like a willow and perfumes the walled garden in June. She had the odd but very effective idea of planting a *Koelreuteria* and a Mount Etna Broom about nine inches apart – presumably in the same hole. They have grown to twenty feet, intertwined, to make a remarkable dome that flowers in July and again in August, turns orange in autumn and yet is evergreen – the acme of arboreal ambivalence.

Perhaps best of all she gave the rectangular walled garden its outlines. We inherited formality to the extent of straight beds all round the walls punctuated with a score of tall clipped *Chamaecyparis lawsoniana* 'Pottenii', and the original notion of apple trees in the lawns pruned to flat mushroom shapes. I have gone further by adding a double line of Irish upright junipers down the centre and anchoring the corners of rectangular centre beds with pyramids of clipped box. Then, within this formal matrix (which really comes into its own in winter), I let the planting rip. I have concentrated on blue, white, pink, silver and cream.

The first real event is a mass of Crown Imperials; then May tulips (especially 'White Triumphator') with euphorbias and mauve *Abutilon*; then pink and white *Eremurus*, yellow Day Lilies with blue veronicas, daphnes, pink, white and blue geraniums; masses of old and Hybrid Musk roses, campanulas, salvias, *Phlox, Agapanthus*, cream kniphofias, Burning Bush, *Clematis* and so on to cream and brown chrysanthemums with the fire of that wonderful dahlia 'Bishop of Llandaff'.

The mood of the walled garden is always (I hope) cheerful, spruce and on parade. My intention is that the water garden is just as positively melancholy and romantic; the 'woods' as sylvan as I can make them; the open glades so pastoral that you can hear the pipes. It is a great deal to ask plants to do. I can't tell whether they manage it or not – my mind's eye has got there already.

Biddick Hall, Chester-le-Street, Co. Durham

Viscount Lambton's Garden

The average middle-aged Englishman and woman have three great affections, their children, their gardens and their dogs. The three have a good deal in common: they all turn out differently from what you expected and all do exactly what you hope they will not. But despite every irritation, they retain their parent's or owner's undiminished affection. I am no exception, so was flattered by the invitation to contribute to this book and with considerable diffidence I accepted, as my wife is both more knowledgeable and a better gardener. I agreed because I would like to make a case for the amateur gardener, which without question I am, having no pretensions to knowledge. I believe that a garden is only successful if it is primarily the work of its owner, and certainly I chose most plants by writing down their names having seen them fully grown in flower, as I have a total inability to know or remember their Latin names, and frequently forget their English ones as well.

Here I think lies the first lesson to gardeners: never stop visiting other gardens. Nothing is so deceptive as a catalogue, nothing so unwise as buying plants without realizing their full potential, so I do not think it is the slightest bit necessary to have a profound knowledge of nomenclature to make a garden. The next thing that should be stressed is the importance of personal taste; nothing is worse than a pure consultant's garden; it is only comparable to a decorator's house, a thing drained of personality, however perfect it may be in detail. The same is true of the gardens of those who frequently take advice; they are a patchwork without cohesion, one idea contradicting another.

My own choice is a formal garden, and I hate the whole trend away from order and the haphazard placing of hideously shaped beds and green spaces without rhyme or reason. Dotted flower beds in gardens are mere expressions of ugliness, disconnected and lost.

Neither have I ever been able to bear 'Surrey delights', pine trees underplanted with heather and boldly coloured azaleas. Is there anything more hideous than an orange azalea? And heather – although I once planted some in error – is surely for grouse, nothing else. Whenever I find myself in one of these gardens I subconsciously find myself looking for golf balls and expect at every turn to find a putting green. Another garden, which some people immensely admire, which I detest is the cluttered garden where plants are piled together as by the house at Hidcote, demanding attention which they now never receive. In fact, Hidcote for me was one unpleasant surprise after another: in trying to be everything, it succeeds in being nothing. You follow an avenue, you find it leads to a turnip field, you go through a formal gate and find yourself in a *Daily Mail* ideal garden, and all the time one is conscious of an American trying to be every type of Englishman.

The reader here may say: but this is merely a destructive list of dislikes. So it is, and it is I believe absolutely essential that these dislikes should be held. Nothing is more irritating than a gardener who will say, 'I dislike that tree but as it is a fine specimen I have left it there.' Such tolerance is the destroyer of cohesion.

But let me turn to my ideal garden: Sissinghurst. A formal garden, yet full of constant surprises, as one garden room leads to another. The Nicolsons created an enchanting entity which leads again and again into itself. Wild plants grown in ordered circumstances achieve the advantages of the two. This ordered disorder and endless intercommunication I tried to follow and went beyond it in planting yew as a more or less continuous background. I cannot understand why yew is considered slow-growing. Give it a little fertilizer and it will shoot away and after a year or two make a foot's growth a year.

91. Lord Lambton's passion for formal planting and his use of topiary are revealed in this bird's-eye view of his garden in Co. Durham.

The death of topiary is one of the saddest things in English gardening, and another is the delusion that yews have to be old to be beautiful. The reverse is the case. Old unpruned yews have great beauty, and an avenue where they reach overhead obscuring all sun, creating a cool world of their own, is a thing of rare romance. But stems of yews of the age of those at Levens lose their foliage and create the effect of rows of inverted corkscrews only admirable to people who love the venerable, twisted and antique. They lose their purpose with their symmetry and compactness. The great advantage of yew is its colour: as a background to roses it has no equal and as a tree it is the one great advantage the English formal garden has over the Italian, as in Italy in summer it loses the special colour which is so perfect here.

The only thing in my garden which could be called original is the creation of the apiary garden. But alas, for some reason or other the box in it is continuously eaten up by rabbits who, when they aren't digging, are making nests for their young. That it should turn out to be a Sargasso sea of rabbit life is I believe bad luck and should not diminish the value of the idea.

One of the delights of old gardens are their utilitarian buildings. How many stables have not been transformed by an elevated dovecote, while the old pigeon houses such as still exist at Chastleton are things of rare beauty: that they have not received better architectural placing is probably due to the appetite of the pigeon. For the hundreds of pigeons which have occupied those houses at their zenith must have caused terrible wars between the pigeon boy and the gardener.

Bees are not like pigeons. They do no harm and hives can be placed in the centre of the garden without the slightest fear, as bees are, unless swarming, most peaceable insects. My four beehives are centrally placed, and in eleven years stingings have been exceedingly rare. Every time I walk through the garden I dwell on the pleasant fallacy that here the decorations are not for show but for economic production of honey. Of course like anything you produce yourself you get the totally erroneous belief that your honey is better than anybody else's. Fishponds too, where they survive, have a rare beauty added to their having a domestic purpose.

But apart from the suggestion that architectural hives could become a feature of informal and formal gardens, I have no suggestion to make except: be ruthless. I have received immense pleasure from this garden, deluding myself that it has moments of great beauty. I know it is a series of adaptations of ideas of others culled from gardens, garden books, architectural plans and prints. To the visitor my pleasure may be a source of scornful pity. If so I do not mind, and certainly the visitor will not, for every gardener will come away happier if he has seen a garden which is clearly inferior to his own.

92. One of the herbaceous borders flanking the formal garden. The square-clipped May trees add the flavour of formality.

93. A pool of blue gentians fill the old rose window taken from Lambton Castle.

94. Even the rose garden has a feeling of formality, with sentinel evergreens and topiaried hedges.

95 (*right*). The Italian garden. A stone and brick path flanked by lead peacocks culminates in a rose-smothered temple.

The Mill House, Corpusty, Norfolk

John and Roger Last's Garden

First of all the house and garden belong to our mother and only one of us brothers is here regularly. We must be grateful for her forbearance in putting up with the upheavals caused by our gardening activities and for her hard work both in the garden and in keeping the property as a whole running.

When we came here in 1947 it was a working mill with a house and garden suffering from the absence of an owner-occupier for nearly half a century. The garden was overgrown with nettles and devoid of cultivated plants, except for snowdrops and the old double daffodil in the neglected orchard; a Horse Chestnut the only large tree.

Although the soil was fertile, it was not a place that appeared to have much potential, sandwiched between a road on one side and a public footpath on the other, the garden almost invisible from the house, encumbered with sheds, pig-sties and a grain store. It was flat and, though near the river, without any natural water. However over the years we have been able to remedy most of these defects.

From the outset we have designed, built, planted and maintained everything ourselves, for the most part working only at weekends. The reclamation has been a slow process, clearing rough ground and removing unwanted buildings bit by bit. This has meant that the garden has developed in sections, which we have tried to link. It was impractical to have an overall plan.

Our main aim has been to grow as wide a variety of plants as possible. To do this we have created a wide range of growing conditions, including a woodland area, a water garden, a dry garden and a rock garden.

Our second aim has been to give the garden a strong architectural backbone. Walls to screen and link, buildings to provide focal points and to enliven, steps, paths and statuary – all combining to give the garden a permanency throughout the seasons.

The main lawn, which followed a year or so of vegetables, was established first. But it was not until the closure of the mill in 1967 that the major expansion of the garden began.

The old orchard was gradually turned into a woodland garden, where the light shade of the remaining apple and pear trees provided ideal conditions for camellias, rhododendrons and magnolias.

This part of the garden is at its best in spring, when the ground is covered with hellebores, mertensias, trilliums, fritillaries and species of peony. *Meconopsis* of various species succeed here, and lilies throughout the summer, including the seven-foot spires of *Cardiocrinum giganteum*.

At the far end of the woodland garden is a mature Horse Chestnut in whose dense shade little would grow, and where the thin hedge exposed the garden to the road. To provide interest in this difficult site we decided a building was needed.

After two winters' work (winter is our building season), having hauled thirty tons of stone the length of the garden in a wheelbarrow, in addition to cement and much other material, the grotto was built.

An entrance passage leads to three circular chambers, each a little deeper into the ground and vaulted with blocks of stone corbelled inwards to a central oculus. The final chamber is lit by an irregular opening looking over the boundary stream to the village common. Two large masks of river gods dominate the central chamber.

The building material was carstone from the quarries of West Norfolk. This is a sandstone the colour of gingerbread, soft at first, but hardening and darkening with exposure, rapidly attracting moss and lichen.

Carstone was used for another building, also built to fill a difficult corner and to provide a focal point at the head of a stream. The gothic ruin is a twenty-foot-high tower, containing a spiral staircase leading to an upper floor which gives views over the surrounding apple trees and the meadow behind. A few years of weathering and the establishment of moss and house leeks has given the ruin an air of antiquity.

The stream which emerges in front of it was once a ditch, but was enlarged to resemble a natural water-course. A channel dug from the river a hundred yards to the north gives a constant flow of water. This finds its way at first through rocks, then widens out through lush vegetation before dropping into a pool. It rejoins the boundary stream after flowing beneath a high bridge built of large round local flints.

96. The only dry part of the garden, this walled and gravelled enclosure provides the right conditions for a collection of plants more suited to arid climates.

Partly shaded and partly in full sunshine, the moist margins of the stream support a rich variety of plants. In the spring come marsh marigolds of various kinds, the tall pink scapes of *Peltiphyllum peltatum* and the vivid yellow spathes of the skunk cabbage, *Lysichitum americanum*. Primulas of many species thrive here, seeding themselves prolifically. Hostas reach an enormous size and also seed themselves, resulting in some interesting varieties. Astilbes, ligularias, rheums, *Zantedeschia aethiopica*, rodgersias, irises and orchids all flourish. Ferns grow in shady areas among boulders of carstone which build up into a cliff twelve feet high, disguising the end wall of the former grain store.

The stream has a second branch which runs from a pool, at the foot of a small terrace. The curved wall behind screens the water garden from the main lawn. The pedimented archway in the wall links lawn and terrace, and is a focal point for both.

Water plays an important part in this garden, for as well as the stream, there are two ponds and some smaller pools, all with fountains. The sound and movement of water, quite apart from the life that it brings, seemed particularly appropriate for the garden of a water mill.

Unfortunately the River Bure on which the mill stands is separated from the garden by a meadow and a public footpath. Only at one point, by the mill pool, does the garden come near the river. By breaching the retaining wall we were able to build steps down to a small garden along one bank. The roaring mill race is only feet away and sometimes this entire area is flooded. Gunneras and Swamp Cypress (*Taxodium distichum*) do well here.

More steps run up to the mill yard. The south-facing mill wall shelters *Abutilon vitifolium*, *Magnolia delavayi* and *Solanum crispum*; roses cover the house, wisteria and *Rosa banksiae* the adjoining stable. Behind the stable and house is the dry garden. A walled enclosure with raised beds provides the sharp drainage essential for the Mediterranean character of the plants grown here. The winter of 1979 gave an early trial to these, but the yuccas, kniphofias, *Cistus*, *Convolvulus cneorum*, *Fremontodendron* 'California Glory' and *Clematis armandii* survived undamaged.

At the far end of this garden is what was formerly a wash-house. By glazing the roof a conservatory was created. Opening up the wall towards the garden, we added a bay with gothick windows and roofed with an ogee dome. Inside, raised beds enclose a pool with a wall fountain, above which is a fine alabaster reredos from a demolished Victorian church.

Because the conservatory is on the north side of the house, it provides ideal conditions for camellias, tree ferns and other plants that thrive in cool but frost-free conditions. Oranges

and oleanders are wintered inside in pots, to be stood on the terrace in front for the summer.

We have found that we can ignore much of the pessimistic advice regarding the cultivation in this part of England of many reputedly tender plants. Norfolk is drier and sunnier than most parts of the country, and the frosts here are not so severe as further inland.

The worst damage comes during the occasional May frost, which blackens many emerging shoots and buds.

The garden naturally is constantly evolving and altering in character. We prefer to adapt our designs as the plants grow rather than forcing them to fit rigidly into the original concept. So gradual change is inevitable, and fortunately we will never finish, for meeting the challenges and opportunities for improvement is what makes the work worthwhile, and our gardening so enjoyable.

John Last   *Roger Last*

97 and 98. Moisture-loving plants thriving on the banks of the stream include giant hostas, astilbes, ligularias and primulas in variety.

99. There is a strong architectural backbone to the garden. Here a pedimented archway links lawn, terrace and low walls. Everywhere there is an abundance of discriminating planting.

100. An attractive high bridge built of large round local flints spans the stream.

Herterton House, Cambo, Northumberland

Frank Lawley's Garden

Herterton House garden began in inspiration in summer 1975, and, physically, a year later. It was an unwanted wilderness around three disused, partly dilapidated old stone buildings, derelict remains of a recently working farmyard. The farmers had moved on, the land had passed to neighbours, the adjacent farmhouse had become the retirement home of a local farming family. The acre of back close with stables, barn, and granary was deserted and rubbish-strewn.

To find a wilderness inside a living garden is depressing, but to foresee the creation of a living garden from a wilderness is inspiring. Such inspiration will sustain one's innocent passage through adversities in manners unthinkable to disinterested bystanders.

It seemed a great chance. After fourteen years of practical garden making, urgent plant collecting, garden visiting, running a nursery . . . it was time to start again.

The previous garden was a cottage garden; Margery Fish was mentor. Thanks to the national urge to constant change – usually in the name of tradition – the riches of the English garden flora are scattered like the spots of the Milky Way. The worst enemy in recent times has been the modern rose, whose insidious spread has overnight emptied entire gardens.

Inspiration also came from the newly replanned, labelled and stocked Wallington Gardens, a delightful walk away through woods bordering the garden. Should a label be missing, one might ask the head gardener, without interrupting work. Once, this dedicated man paused and said that, for him, the tree was the noblest of nature's creations, and principal adornment of a garden. I was amazed. In those woods, I knew a carpet of wintergreen, a bank of Asarabacca, variegated elder, hedgehog holly, sites of green orchids, black burdocks and white comfreys, and nothing of the trees.

From the garden of black soil, incongruously sheltered by woods conceived as great garden architecture two and a half centuries ago, we are transplanted to truly wild Northumberland. Sharp contours of hills, rocky outcrops, fingers of forest, curves of rivers bridged for sheep, and all-pervading green, perhaps fancifully recall Capability Brown, who travelled the same hills attending school, and starting work.

This garden will be an English country garden. Small well-ordered compartmented gardens meeting all needs, medicinal, culinary, aesthetic, were common two or three centuries ago. They were practical developments from earlier 'green room' extensions to busy, overcrowded, polluted houses, which, with secluded enclosures, secret seats, 'alleys', and contrasting plains of brilliant sculptured flower patterns, offered escape to peace, privacy and stimulating aesthetic delight.

Further incentive to considered design and planting, rather than dabbling improvisations, came from a growing appreciation of oriental rugs, the indoor winter gardens of the mythical inventors of gardening.

Though the site was rich in grass, nettle and dock, hopes of speedy conversion soon evaporated. Initial fork proddings touched stone, but how much there was could never have been imagined. After sodium chlorate, a man rich in machines and ideas was engaged to de-stone, level and rotavate.

Remaining soil and sub-soil were evenly spread, supplemented with hundreds of tons of peat locally dug, manure, sand and gravel. Joy at seeing the first levelling was dashed when early winter rains turned all to mud. Patches of creamy clay, exposed like raw nerves in ploughing, held wellingtons like vices; lakes formed and stayed. The entire second spit had to be manually excavated, clay and boulders removed, drains repaired, paths filled with stone. Helped by good

101. The Weeping Silver Pear tree on a mounded circular bed of silver periwinkle 'Joy-of-the-Ground' is the herb garden's centrepiece.

102. Part of the front formal garden. Gold-variegated London Pride edges the topiary beds; patches of golden Creeping Jenny, in front of box hedges, cover Crown Imperials and early lilies; low-walled beds of Snow in Summer and Rock Cress make white lacy tablecloths.

103. Looking through honeysuckle into the herb garden in early summer when bed-edgings of dwarf, deep pink London Pride are in full flower. Silver wormwood is in the foreground; common wormwood and different southernwoods occupy other square corner beds.

104. An ancient carved-stone water pot in a small flower bed, planted in many shades of pink.

relatives, half a dozen 'Job Creation' boys and girls, and the gallant Northumbria Conservationists, the work took three years.

With no existing features, we could indulge in clean sheets of paper on drawing boards. Paper planning inspires; colour effects can be filled in with crayons. Count paces to get proportions correct. The best tip received for laying out was to tie string as tightly as possible between posts to level intervening land – checking regularly that rains or straying boots had not slackened it. Edging stones were laid on sand marked by strings, paths measured two or four feet wide.

Different areas were parts formed according to the initial vision. After years exiled in boxes, pots and vegetable allotments, the surviving plants began to arrive.

First planted was the front 'formal' garden. After box and gold-variegated London Pride for edging, and box and yew for clipping, spaces were given full cottage treatment. As our most respectful visits to Levens Hall should have told us, that was wrong. The desires to re-create favourite effects had to be disciplined.

It was agreed that generally there should be no repetition, each garden having its own policy and personality. The favourite native evergreens, box, holly, yew and ivy, are in most parts, and are the basic shrub ingredients. Pink and yellow, as the Impressionists taught, are the colours of

sunshine, and are near all warm domestic walls. Perfect in flower are *Lonicera caprifolium* and 'glory' rose, 'Gloire de Dijon', and in foliage, golden yew, 'Buttercup' ivy, *Lonicera* 'Baggesen's Gold' and *L. japonica* 'Aureo-reticulata', which share the house front. White and grey-green are for shade. The walk from the front, through the herb garden to the rear courtyard from which you enter the flower and nursery gardens, has its foot in shadow by the time most people see it, and is edged in greeny cream 'white' *Corydalis*.

The herb garden is a simple knot with pairs of pentagons recalling granary arches, and a central circle for the Silver Willow-Leaf Pear. Square corner beds have wormwoods and southernwoods. Dye and medicinal plants mingle in a garden of scent. In small beds, sweet thymes and carnations contrast with rues and hyssops, and in deeper borders, camphor, tansy and mugwort mingle with daphnes, mock orange, rose and lavender. The culinary salad garden is separate, within the nursery.

You enter the flower garden through a low gate in a high stone wall. Here are most of our dearest plants. The ten-month or more wait to renew acquaintance with the buttercups – single and double Fair Maids of France, and Bachelors' Buttons (*Ranunculus aconitifolius* and *R. acris* 'Flore Pleno') – is worthwhile. Their colours are indelible marks on the face of the season's clock. No labour-saving evergreen

90

105. Looking north into the flower garden. In the near bed, unlit in winter, small-leaved weeping box, fingered ivy, creeping hard fern, and Miss Jekyll's dwarf white periwinkle make a green frame for the flowers beyond.

106. The pale-pink flowered golden-leaved phlox, and, beyond on the left, a locally found deep blue sea holly, *Eryngium spinalba*.

ground covers can replace them, though it is essential to keep the droves of old pansies and carpets of thrifts for lasting company as the prima donnas pass by.

The sun-followers tend to look at us, since the aspect from the house is to the north. The effect should be of a place full of flowers; not quite the nature garden of Monet's poppy-fields, nor the exquisite flower meadows of Botticelli, but a clearly defined enclosure edged with shrubs and walls through which one can wander, knee-deep in flowers. Beds are shallow and strewn with stepping stones; you can be quite familiar with your lilies. The great magnificence of Jekyll borders with graded heights and colours would seem hostile here.

To define the character of our flowers? 'Cottage', 'old-fashioned'? Better not be too tight. There are the sharp-eyed discoveries of unusual forms of wild plants: white water avens, blue wood anemones, double ditch campions and Lady's Smock, variegated white thyme, purple elderberry. And, ever discoverable, equally rare garden mutations. Our rarest is gold variegated phlox with palest pink flowers. No latest breeders' hybrids, nor distant travelling hunters' trophies, but I admit to collecting some older florists' creations – pompom chrysanths, pinks like 'Dad's Favourite', and the tiny seventeenth-century *Rosa* 'Burgundica'.

If one could have just a handful, quite simple plants come to mind: double white *Arabis*, rich purple Peal of Bells (*Campanula glomerata*), Coral Cowslips (*Pulmonaria rubra*), Hen and Chickens Daisy who waits, tantalizing, till the very end of daisy time before producing her brood, and last, turquoise Shamrock Pea (*Parochetus communis*).

The shrub maze offers complete contrast, curving paths, closed vistas, shade. Box, *Berberis* and *Cotoneaster* give density, variegated hawthorns and buddleias lighter effects. The path winds through the high wall into the nursery, where long thin beds fill and refill twice a year.

There is still lots to do, and many thoughts to think. Time will prune our efforts and establish our architecture. Will our walls and nourished hollies check uninhibited winds sweeping from greater heights to north and west? We still all seek to create our Garden of Eden where, among our birds and flowers, working in all seasons, we renew our ties with nature. To feel one's own back as a sundial, one's head as pointer, marked by the sun's passage through the day, confirms one's knowledge of commitment.

Frank Lawley

91

Great Dixter, Northiam, Sussex

Christopher Lloyd's Garden

In two interrelated ways I have been extremely lucky in my gardening life. First, my parents were both gardening enthusiasts in their different ways and they somehow transmitted this to me, so that I cannot remember the time when I was not enthralled. Second, I was born to a garden whose framework was already made.

Perhaps it would have been good for me to have had to struggle against a seemingly hopeless tangle of scrub, overcrowded trees, brambles and nettles and to have emerged triumphant with my own brand of order wrested from chaos. Other contributors to this volume achieved just that, I know, but I do not envy them. It is soothing to be born with a silver spoon on your plate, and it has very different contents now from when it was first laid out in 1912.

My father bought Great Dixter, a fifteenth-century half-timbered manor house, in 1910. Except for a summertime tenant it had been empty for ten years and there was no garden; just a couple of orchards, a yucca, a bay tree, a wild pear and a fig. But there were a number of lovely farm buildings – all roofed with warm red tiles encrusted on their sunny slopes with grey and yellow lichens. These were marvellous features to incorporate into a garden design and the work was done by Lutyens, who also restored and added to the house. He never worked with Jekyll here; she had nothing to do with the place. I wish I could lay that misconception, so often repeated in print.

The garden was laid out in a semi-formal style with beautiful York stone paths (horribly slippery when wet), culled from London's newly asphalted pavements, and lies all around the house, the one never out of sight of the other. House and garden are delightfully integrated.

My father was a good designer and made our sunk garden in 1923. He was immensely interested in the art of topiary. Castellated hedging and groups of topiary figures, nearly all in yew, are a feature here. He was good at carpentry too; I am hopeless at any kind of precision work. So although I like the topiary as being part of the place I have never re-created it where pieces have died nor cherished it quite as it deserves, which is on my conscience. Not that I am sorry I replaced a boring ball-and-saucer yew in our front lawn with the strange (some think repulsive) Chilean bamboo, *Chusquea culeou*. That gives me satisfaction.

My mother was the plantsman (I baulk at the hideous plantsperson and plantswoman sounds silly). She appreciated the art of letting plants enjoy themselves in unplanned ways. Self-sown seedlings – for instance of *Daphne mezereum* or *Lilium regale* – were quickly spotted and treasured. She would go round the garden with a trugful of snowdrop bulbs or of cyclamen seedlings together with some nice potting soil to make them comfortable and pop them into all sorts of odd places; under the skirts of hedges and topiary specimens, into paving and wall cracks.

This very personal approach is what gives to all private gardens, where the owners are deeply involved, a living identity, highly charged, idiosyncratic, absolutely genuine (*echt* was the German word my mother loved to use), each one unique. And it is this that visitors to private gardens so much enjoy: the feeling that the place is loved and lived in, even if it is not one hundred per cent organized and tidy.

If you love your garden in this way you will love the plants in it and they will be richly assorted. There must be thousands of different kinds at Dixter (nearly all unlabelled! – the labels have been written, but where's the time to put them out?). I think the garden combines the ideal of a firm framework with informal planting.

I do use bedding plants. In fact the art of combining them in different ways, which you can practise twice (or even three times) in every year without ever repeating yourself, I find endlessly fascinating. And yet there are no beds of which the visitor could say: 'There's his bedding out.' It is blended into the borders with more permanent background features.

Even the rose garden, which (albeit in a charming design on the site of an old cattle yard) still follows the stereotyped concept of setting the roses aside in beds devoted to them alone, has developed a very different aspect from what the rosarian would expect or approve. Each bed used to be devoted to one or two varieties of Hybrid Teas with two of them given over to Bourbons and Hybrid Perpetuals. When 'La Tosca' and 'Prince de Bulgarie' went out of fashion they were replaced by 'Mme Butterfly', then all the rage, and when that began to totter I suppose it should have been replaced by 'Prima Ballerina', but I had come along by then. I still like 'Mme Butterfly' and where she has remained healthy I have left her but filled the gaps with other roses whose colours do not jar and that I have raised from cuttings from friends' gardens. So much more fun. Some of the bushes are seventy years old – H.P.s brought by my parents from their first garden – while others have only just been added. And there are clematis on poles in among 'Mme Isaac Pereire' and her like; *Verbena bonariensis* and wild teasels seed

themselves here and there and that charming (I think so anyway, though Will Ingwersen adjures us to avoid it like the plague) coppery leaved *Oxalis* with yellow flowers making itself at home in the bed margins and interlocking with scented white violets. It all adds up to a living tapestry.

There were very few shrubs in the garden when it was first planted. The Long Border, for instance, was all herbaceous for its seventy yards length and five yards depth with just a group of white *Magnolia denudata* at the lower end, which is still there. Everything else, apart from one old clump of the Tree Scabious, *Cephalaria gigantea*, has changed. I've put in lots of shrubs, most of them notable for good foliage which sustains you through a long season. And it's a good place for certain roses of no special merit for shapeliness.

I've even included trees: there's a group with Dickson's Golden Elm, the very pale grey-leaved willow *Salix alba argentea, Eucalyptus perriniana* and a green-and-white-variegated Sweet Chestnut, *Castanea sativa*, but all are restricted to step-ladder height by pruning.

I have retained plenty of herbaceous plants to give me large splashes of colour, notably border phloxes and *Monarda* 'Cambridge Scarlet', which love my heavy soil. The border's

107. Surrealist shapes in the mist, the topiary was originally the creation of Christopher Lloyd's father, Nathaniel, who bought Great Dixter in 1910.

main season is mid-June to mid-August, but wherever I can extend it without weakening the effect, I have done so.

What Arthur Hellyer calls two-tier planting is an excellent plan. For instance the white *Allium neapolitanum* and the large-headed *A. christophii* flower in May–June but can be inter- or underplanted – with *Sedum* 'Ruby Glow', flowering in August–September. Snowdrops and violets can colonize the foot of deciduous shrubs like roses and *Weigela florida* 'Variegata'. Tulips can be interplanted with fairly static colonies of *Rudbeckia* 'Goldsturm' and Japanese Anemones or with grey-foliage plants like *Santolina* and *Senecio cineraria* that can be cut hard back when the tulips need light and space. Forget-me-nots seed themselves among the phloxes to make a mist of blue before the border has filled up.

The Long Border is fronted by a nice broad straight-flagged path. Then comes a strip of mown grass before you are in the complete informality of the orchard.

This is just one of a number of areas of meadow garden which deserves a word more before I sign off. They are a special part of Dixter and appeal to or repel the public according to their upbringing. 'Your lawns are weedy' is the not unexpected reaction of some, when they see areas of long grass tossed this way and that by rain and wind. We seldom give these areas their first cut before the last week in July, and do most of the cutting in August, because I want all their contents, like fritillaries, camassias and wild orchids, to ripen and shed their seeds so that the tissue of colour which they comprise is increased and intensified under its own momentum, having been given a start by initial plantings. This is what is meant by naturalizing plants. Given the right setting it is a lovely relaxed form of gardening and it creates a home for many plants that modern systems of farming have made quite rare in the wild.

Christopher Lloyd

108. The Long Border leading up to the fifteenth-century house is a popular feature of the garden in summer.

109. The octagonal lily pond in the sunk garden originally created in 1923. The formal structure contrasts happily with the relaxed planting.

110. Plants in the moat meadow gardens are allowed to naturalize. Self-sown Snakeshead Fritillaries, primroses and wild orchids flourish.

111. The pleated leaves and spiky flowers of *Veratrum album* and *Hosta ventricosa* 'Variegata' contrast strongly in this border detail.

The Quinta, Swettenham, Cheshire

Sir Bernard Lovell's Garden

When I returned to my post in the University of Manchester after the war I had no idea that my life was soon to revolve around a region known as Jodrell Bank in Cheshire. By 1948 my commitment to Jodrell had become inescapable and we searched for a house in the countryside near the growing telescopes. One morning in May fate led us to the small village of Swettenham, ten minutes drive from Jodrell, but only three hours from the time when The Quinta was to be auctioned, and before the end of that afternoon the former rectory and stables, together with a few acres of pasture, were ours.

The garden was unexciting. Our predecessors had wanted the minimum garden and maximum meadow for their daughter's pony – we were to move in the opposite direction, taking in more and more of the fields to the south and west as the years passed. After two years we had absorbed the immediate problems and hired an earth-scoop to move the drive fifty yards away from the house. It was the first of what were to be nine expansions towards the present garden of about ten acres, and it is these additions over intervals of years, often with shelter belts planted on the successive boundaries, that have determined the shape and nature of the garden today.

The turn in from the lane is marked by a group of *Populus trichocarpa* purchased in 1952 for a few pence and now towering fifty feet or more above all else in the immediate vicinity. In the earliest days of spring the banks of the drive are smothered in snowdrops – an early sackful contained some *Galanthus plicatus* and these are spreading faster than *G. nivalis*. There is a line of cherries on one side of the drive and larch on the other. In April there is a tunnel of blossom and the new green of the larch and then the carpet of petals in May and of the leaves in autumn are recurrent annual pleasures.

The region immediately south of the drive contains some of our earliest plantings. We soon found that the acid sandy soil and the climate suited birch and sorbus. In fact, the common birch is the most prevalent seedling and we have collected every variety of birch we can find. Fortunately in that first plantation in 1956 we had *Betula papyrifera* and a number of Japanese birches and these are now mature specimens. So too is a *Phellodendron amurense*, which, with its corky bark, is often a puzzle for visitors, a Dawyck Beech which becomes a pillar of fire in the autumn, and a *Parrotia persica* which helps to cheer the winter scene.

The original boundary on the west with cows grazing only a few yards from the kitchen window was far too close for comfort. Fortunately it was glebe land and we were able to acquire another acre. Eventually in 1966 we purchased the whole glebe field, but the succession of three boundaries and shelter belt planting, mainly *Pinus sylvestris* and *P. nigra*, has determined the sequence of the lawn and plantation in that direction. Nearest the house and bordering the drive there is the Willow Tree lawn named for the *Salix* 'Chrysocoma' (1953) but dominated today by two magnificent cherries, *Prunus* 'Shirotae' ('Mt Fuji'); the other, purchased as *P.* 'Shirofugen', fortunately turned out to be the Double Gean *P. avium* 'Plena', a marvellous pyramid of blossom in the spring. At the original north-east boundary only yards from the kitchen window there was an aged thorn tree which puzzled us because half of it behaved like an ordinary hawthorn whereas the other half was almost evergreen with early blossom. After a few years we realized that the 'ordinary' half was the sucker from a graft of the Glastonbury Thorn, *Crataegus monogyna* 'Biflora'. Now, the latter stands gnarled and resplendent, blossoming on Christmas Day.

Indeed, every Christmas Day my occupation is to tour the

garden and list the flowers discernible – never less than two or three dozen, because we have made a determined effort to give some colour close to the house throughout the winter. In December and January the kitchen window is confronted by the thorn, to the north groups of *Mahonia* 'Charity' and *Viburnum bodnantense*. Then, seen across the kitchen garden a *Salix acutifolia* 'Blue Streak', which with its early silver catkins against a dark background of the shelter belt is a colourful sight. On the 'island' around which the drive turns, there are witch hazels, but perhaps the most exciting is the Chinese cherry, *Prunus conradinae*. Planted in 1954 this is now a large tree and in February covered in blossom, changing from slight pink to white. Although we have plenty of tits they do not seem to spoil the cherries and thus all through the winter we can see from our windows *Prunus subhirtella* 'Autumnalis' and, at the turn of the year, *P. incisa* 'Praecox'.

Frequently some national or family event has been the reason or the excuse for planting or layout. The arrival of twins in 1951, increasing our young family to five, was celebrated by two chestnuts planted where the drive bends towards the house.

Another event (my Reith Lectures in 1959) was marked by the planting of an avenue of Red-Twigged Limes curving across the remainder of the three-acre meadow. This is Reith Avenue. To the south of this during the next five or six years we planted steadily. Not everything survived, but amongst the successes has been the Bhutan Pine (*Pinus wallichiana*), always beautiful with its long pendulous needles but especially so in May when the long upright 'candles' of new growth emerge. Nearby, the catkins of the Musk Willow from Armenia (*Salix aegyptiaca*) are vivid against a blue February sky. Amongst the other conifers in that area the Weymouth Pine, *Pinus strobus*, and the Greek Fir, *Abies cephalonica*, have grown well. At the eastern end an orchard interplanted with a variety of crabs provides fruit for the house, the material for delicious jellies, as well as the beauty of flower and leaf.

Whereas Reith Avenue curved away to the south, another event early in 1961 gave us the excuse for the long east–west avenue of Lombardy Poplars, *Populus nigra* 'Italica' – Knight's Avenue – which for some time formed the northern boundary of that area. It was at this stage that we embarked on our most hazardous enterprise. We had no water in the garden, so in February of 1961 we hired a bulldozer and excavated the area between the two avenues for a small lake. A few months later our geologist son, home on vacation from Oxford, assured us that the water would immediately disappear through the sand. He was right, and we soon gazed upon a dry pit and a huge mound of excavated sand. We consulted the owner of an ancient water mill in the village

who, in colourful language, told us what to do. So hundreds of tons of clay had to be imported and puddled with gumboot and spade. It was a formidable task and no child or visitor escaped duty. Eventually after two years of hard labour we achieved our ambition and today, surrounded by dogwoods and willows and with the banks covered with primroses, and with mallard and moorhen our companions, the area never fails to fascinate.

A wide grass ride curls from the lake north-eastwards towards the church tower. East and west of this ride we continued our plantings. There *Eucalyptus gunnii* is a huge triple-trunk tree; and in that collection *Tilia* 'Petiolaris', *Crataegus tanacetifolia*, *Acer rufinerve* (one of many handsome

112. In 1959 Sir Bernard gave the B.B.C. Reith Lectures and this avenue of limes – Reith Avenue – was planted beside the lake in commemoration.

snake-bark maples), *Sorbus folgneri, Fraxinus velutina, Alnus incana* and many others have grown into substantial trees. The walk down the ride to the lake is never without interest, be it the beauty of the spring morning with the *Acer* and whitebeam leaves unfolding or the starkness of winter when the boles of *Eucalyptus niphophila, Acer capillipes, Salix pentandra*, or the shapes of the *Nothofagus* dominate.

The Queen's jubilee, coinciding with a fortunate local circumstance, at last enabled us to fulfil a long-felt want – to push out further to the west so that we could reach the steep banks where we overlook the winding River Dane. We continued the curving line of Reith Avenue past a magnificent oak, at least two hundred years old, to widen out into Jubilee Ride bordered by *Populus* 'Tacatricho 32' (for rapid growth because we want to see them catch up with the limes).

Now we have a garden in which paths wind through the trees and shrubs with the flowers of spring in the undercover. In the summer, roses and clematis smother the house walls and many of the trees. Apart from the avenues and shelter belts there is little repetition. Fortunately there is an index of the plantings and that already contains a few thousand items – many now grown from seed collected on our journeys to other places. If we were planning those ten acres now, much would be different – but the garden has grown over three decades and the successive areas enclosed are evocative of the events of our family life since we first glimpsed this Cheshire village on that fortunate day in May in 1948. Now it is the place where the unending changes of flora and fauna provide, as Francis Bacon wrote of gardens three and a half centuries ago, the purest of human pleasures.

Bernard Lovell

113 (*above left*). A good specimen of *Eucalyptus gunnii*, one of several *Eucalyptus* species thriving in this garden.

114. A strong display of *Lonicera × americana* on the north-facing wall of the courtyard at The Quinta.

115 (*above right*). The south-west corner of the house, dominated by the Moroccan broom *Cytisus battandieri*, with *Carpenteria californica* to the right. The rose on the wall is 'Caroline Testout'. The small shrub to the left is *Hebe rakaiensis. Akebia quinata, Campsis radicans* and *Jasminum officinale* are also on the wall.

116. The lake at The Quinta with the left bank covered in dogwoods.

Bracken Hill, Platt, Kent

David McClintock

Keys to how this garden has evolved are space and time. It covers three acres, practically none of which can be left to nature, although wild life is encouraged, except for rabbits, squirrels and moles. In the thirty-six years we have been here, I have had endless other commitments as well as a full-time job, and garden help has been uncertain and inexpert. So the only way to make a presentable show generally was to create a 'wild' garden that would look after itself. That means no cosseting, no watering, no staking, no spraying, no pruning, ideally no weeding even; and only suited, healthy plants will survive this. Fortunately, many do.

We are on the brow of a waterless hill facing east-south-east but well sheltered with evergreens. The natural soil is mostly thin acid sand with a hard pan a short way down. There are glorious 180-year-old oaks, and superb birches of exceptional height – over seventy-five feet – which give dappled shade, and an inherited framework of Lawson Cypresses about as tall, and other conifers, notably a Deodar and a Wellingtonia, which may have been the first to have its outer bark scratched off by the squirrels.

There is considerable variation in what will cover the ground more decoratively than the drabber constituents of natural vegetation and still be trouble-free. Some local natives are very acceptable, for example Meadow Saxifrage, Herb Robert, Pignut, Yellow Pimpernel, Ground Ivy with deep pink flowers, Ox-eye Daisies. The essential consideration is that everything introduced must be able to oust, or keep at bay, the duller native plants, mostly coarse grasses, that belong in such conditions; and what succeeds will be different in sun and shade, in drier to less dry places, from one aspect to another.

Away from shade, the heathers are supreme, never, never, pruned, forming dense often deep thickets of intermingling sorts, completely weed-free soon after they have joined up,

colourful with flowers or foliage, or both, at all times of the year, in great variety. Some are very unusual, some original plants of now well-known cultivars. The only trouble is that they do so well that we are always seeking other plants to make a change, but nothing else does quite so well for so long. Cistuses and Brooms are too large and the latter do only too well. We have two special ones here, the *indefessus* form of Common Broom (*The Garden*, January 1978), which has a second flowering in August, which lingers on for months, complementing the invaluable Gorse, and the Spanish *Cytisus striatus* with its sleek grey-striated stems, now naturalized on roadsides in Britain and France (*The Garden*, October 1981).

Some grasses make a tolerable matrix in which are naturalized thousands of daffodils and other bulbs, and plants with creeping 'roots', anathema in borders, such as Great and Lesser Stitchworts, Cypress Spurge, mints and some Michaelmas Daisies. When unwanted perennials have been removed, herbaceous plants can make themselves so much at home that few weeds manage to re-enter. A whole host which happen to like our surroundings have been used this way, for instance Lenten Roses, columbines, *Thalictrum minus*, Epimediums, *Pachyphragma macrophyllum*, Dame's Violet, many geraniums, *Erodium manescavi*, *Rubus tricolor*, the delightful *Epilobium hirsutum* f. *albo-roseum* (*The Garden*, March 1980), *Chaerophyllum aureum*, far better than the native *Anthriscus sylvestris*, Sweet Cicely, *Smyrnium perfoliatum*, *Euphorbia hyberna*, *Lysimachia punctata*, *Trachystemon orientale*, *Pentaglottis sempervirens*, pulmonarias, *Echium rosulatum*, a totally hardy long-flowering Iberian endemic, *Acanthus spinosus*, *Senecio tanguticus*, *Doronicum pardalianches*, the delightful pink *Achillea asplenifolia*, and the bright early grass *Melica uniflora* f. *albida*, true from seed. Under and by an oak above the lawn, the self-perpetuating succession is:

good daffodils, Woad, a speciality of the garden, wild Foxgloves, verbascums, notably *V. virgatum*, and white *Lychnis chalcedonica*, their grey leaves lasting through the winter. Giant Hogweeds are essential architectural plants, decking statelily wherever they are allowed to appear. For barer places, *Montia parvifolia* f. *flagellaris, Cerastium decalvans* mixing elegantly with coloured ajugas, and *Veronica fruticulosa* promise well. Bluebells grow almost too widely: primroses diminishing, cause unknown.

I could go on and on, but must specially mention Comfreys and Polygonums. *Symphytum ibiricum* (*grandiflorum*) makes exemplary cover and adds early brick-red buds. The stout plant with china-blue flowers we used to call *S. caucasicum* is excellent, better than true *caucasicum*, which, with several others, fits into the tapestry.

Polygonum campanulatum is the queen of the genus – about ten sorts here, a great drift of its pink flowers lasting from summer to the frosts, a complete weed-suppressor. *P. molle* is a delight too, not the least with its shining fruits like blackcurrants on pink stalks: *Fagopyrum dibotrys* rivals it with its long-lasting white plumes atop eight-foot stems. But the most elegant of all is *P. lichiangense* – fat pink stems, apple-green leaves and white flowers.

Dozens of shrubs join in the array. There are several distinct seedlings from *Berberis darwinii* × *B. linearifolia* (*B.* × *lologensis*), *Genista aetnensis* (self-seeds), *Cytisus battandieri* (seeded once), *Skimmia laureola, Eucryphia* × *intermedia* 'Rostrevor', *Kalmia angustifolia* both white and pink, *Osmanthus delavayi*, a huge *O. burkwoodii* and *Embothrium coccineum*. *Cotoneaster simonsii* is really a weed, but produces rich autumn colour. I reckon however the loveliest is *Salix acutifolia*, above all when it is swaying in the breeze like a most graceful palm.

Darker, shadier places are lightened with *Hedera colchica* 'Dentata Variegata', Gardener's Garters, *Anaphalis yedoensis* and white Honesty, especially important in winter. Ordinary Irish Ivy can be useful too – a root from here gained an A.M. in 1980. Deep shade, for example under an old yew, is coloured all the year round by *Lamium galeobdolon* 'Variegatum' (no nuisance here), and bespangled for many weeks on end by white and pink *Montia sibirica. M. perfoliata* is usefully allowed there too.

Thickets of *Spiraea douglasii* and of *S.* × *billiardii* 'Triumphans' are dull but douse everything, except bracken. The Azalea grove is another weed-free area, most of it the common, very fragrant yellow. Under part of it, and into the grass, the American form of May Lily makes a close carpet, lit in May with countless small candles.

A considerable part of the upper garden was dense rhododendron with quiet, sunken paths underneath, and off them 'houses' for, now, grandchildren. Some of these rhodies are fine 'Britannia' hybrids, but most are 'ponticums', which are gradually being replaced. Here again, no weeds.

There are groves too of common-or-garden bamboos, *Pseudosasa japonica* (as we are going to have to call *Arundinaria j.*), inherited, and now cleaned out to reveal cool soft weedless clearings. Books say bamboos need moisture, but that they never get here and they still reach seventeen feet. The main grove has been extended with other species to make an evergreen area of varying textures, *Sasaella ramosa* (*Arundinaria vagans* to most of us), firmly imprisoned by stainless steel sheets. Elsewhere plastic strips keep wide-creeping weeds at bay invisibly. Quite a number of other bamboos are grown, from dwarfs upwards, some from seed. The sunny *Pleioblastus* (*Arundinaria*) *viridistriatus* (*variegata*) is perfectly happy in grass, *Chusquea* is full of character; but the loveliest of all is *Thamnocalamus* (*Arundinaria*) *falconeri*, three exuberant clumps in different places, taken from afar by some visitors for Weeping Willows.

Near the house, domesticity demands proper flower beds, which are in any event needed for numerous smaller or special plants – the rockery stretches for over twenty yards, all at breast height or above, thanks to being on a hillside. In these beds, and elsewhere as opportunity offers, other weed-inhibiting plants are used. Some are natives, such as Heath Bedstraw, Maiden Pink and the usually unrecognized *Potentilla* × *mixta*, but the Japanese *P. centigrana* can be good too. 'Weeds' there may be, but mostly unusual ones, rare British plants (some conserved as almost, if not quite, extinct in our islands). So I tend to be a too unwilling weeder of them. Perhaps the liveliest are the annual Rock Rose *Tuberaria guttata* and the Catchfly *Silene gallica* f. *quinquevulnera* with a crimson mark on each of its five white petals, some say like a Sweet William. Two happy mixtures in these beds are, by chance, the annual *Sedum cepaea*, 'Silver Queen' thyme, Hidcote Lavender and *Corydalis lutea*, and purple-leaved *Plantago major* with *Calamintha sylvatica*. A successful weed-suppressing bed is of a *Romneya* with a prickly calyx (*R. trichocarpa* or × *hybrida*?) preceded by *Allium stipitatum*.

This is a varied and storeyed collection, used for study too, which seems to appeal to more than the addict or specialist plantsman.

David McClintock.

117. Colourful with flowers or foliage, at all times of the year heathers are a speciality of David McClintock's garden. In the background a variant of the Common Broom *Cytisus indefessus*, collected in Brittany, is very long-flowering.

118. It is customary to cut back the smaller, lower heathers; but here the heathers are always left unpruned. The rockery is dominated by the massive bulk of *Erica erigena* 'Superba', perhaps the tallest example known.

119. A dense carpet of *Geranium macrorrhizum*. From the sweetly scented leaves is derived the Oil of Geranium of commerce.

120. The split-log bridge over the ditch adds charm. The rare white *Kalmia angustifolia candida* and *Kalmia angustifolia rubra* grow alongside *Athyrium filix-femina friʒelliae*.

121. A view of the garden near the lower pond.

Larch Wood, Beachamwell, Norfolk

Maurice Mason's Garden

In 1947 I was a tenant farmer on a large estate where the landlord had died and to pay the death duties my farm and 100 acres of woodland were to be sold. I wanted to retain my farm so I had to buy both. After the deal had been completed I went to look at the woodland, trisected by roads into forty, thirty and thirty acres. They were very, very untidy, having been used as an army dump during the war.

As a first step we took out all the old iron and junk in the larger area and then all the dying trees. This seemed to take a long while. Then we began to plant the more or less normal forestry trees in fairly regular rows.

I found that I was becoming attracted to this area and built a small chalet where we could have lunch and sit and look at what was going on. Then we started putting in decorative trees and shrubs up the various rides.

I should explain that this area is absolutely typical Norfolk Breckland, which is sand over gravel over chalk, and with a very low rainfall averaging about 23 inches per year.

The years went by and we became more and more attracted to Larch Wood, so we enlarged the chalet and made it into a bungalow where we now live. At the same time our old garden at Fincham had become grossly overcrowded and having this apparently irresistible urge to put plants into the ground we started clearing out some of the forestry trees and replacing them with things we liked, or, when we could, things which didn't already grow at Fincham. We found, again very much to our surprise, that the tiny little *Narcissus cyclamineus* and *N. bulbocodium* would flower here perfectly happily although I think it has taken four to five years from seed. Almost all the other bulbs we put in the grass have been very happy.

Then, one day a few years ago, I was in the Edinburgh Botanic Garden where the Curator explained they had propagated many ericas and did not know what to do with

them. I asked him if I could have some and was promptly given three or four thousand plants, which formed the nucleus of a heather garden which, to my mind, is now one of the more attractive features of the place. We had a problem with rabbits at the start but put a net round the whole wood and have virtually eliminated them. I mention this because the rabbits were in the habit of chewing the heathers right down to the ground. On reflection I do not think this did them harm as it made them nice, tight, compact plants.

On 2 January 1976, there was a tremendous gale, which took out about 350 trees, large and small, and presented us with quite a problem. First we had to get the tops out, then the trunks and finally, where we could, the stumps. Fortunately it made a great deal more space for planting, which was a blessing in disguise, although I rather wished the wind had been more selective in what it took.

All the roses do fairly well down here and, except for the bore of pulling the suckers out, they are comparatively trouble-free. They certainly give good value over a long period and, in many cases, when the flowers have gone, provide a brilliant crop of hips.

Autumn colour on chalk is usually not too good or reliable but there are a few plants we can rely on, the Norway Maple being one of the best. *Photinia villosa* is another plant guaranteed to give a good show and so are some of the better-known *Prunus* species.

I suppose, though, that the joy of Larch Wood in the autumn is the very large collection of sorbus species we have amassed over the years. We say we have eighty or ninety different species and cultivars and I love them all. They like our dry, rather chalky conditions and other than honey fungus are trouble-free. Honey fungus I'm afraid is something that we have got all over the wood and we must learn

122. An autumn view showing part of the extensive collection of slow-growing conifers.

to live with it. Whenever a tree or a shrub dies we promptly put another back in the hole from which the first one came and I have yet to see the second one killed. It is too big an area to treat.

Hollies, too, which are another great favourite of ours, although slow, have succeeded well and in the years to come should make magnificent specimens. Fortunately, with the wood being so sandy and dry we are able to drive all round it and get within fifteen feet of any plant. For someone who is growing older this is a very attractive feature and every evening, when the nights are light, my wife and I get in the car to go and look at something which appeals to us.

A great friend gave us *Cardiocrinum giganteum* var. *yunnanense* which I did not think would like us. Much to our surprise they do, provided we put an enormous quantity of farmyard manure under them.

Camellias are too tender and get too knocked about with the frost to be worthwhile. It is sad because I would grow them for their foliage even if they never flowered.

There is, as such, no formal gardening except for a little bit round the bungalow, where we keep all the small plants which might get lost if they were put further afield.

We have made a collection of slow-growing conifers, which are really rather fun although of course a number of them are not, in the end, very small. The larger conifers are never going to be very exciting here because there is too much wind and not enough rain. They survive but they never look very happy and I wouldn't much care if they all came out.

A number of magnolias have done surprisingly well and the quickest growers are certainly the Gresham hybrids which we put in three or four years ago. *Magnolia grandiflora*, standing free, is slowly making a rounded bush and the clone 'Maryland' flowers when it is very young and over a long season. The other different varieties of *grandiflora* are only just now beginning to be worthwhile. *Magnolia kobus* and M. *salicifolia* are perfectly happy and in course of time will make big plants. We have raised seedlings from them to

123. A blue sky and evergreens create a splendid contrast for autumn foliage.

124. Over ninety species and cultivars of *Sorbus* grow here. This is *Sorbus vilmorinii* in autumn.

125. The attractive autumn berries of *Euonymus europaeus* 'Red Cascade'.

126. *Euonymus radicans coloratus* makes an extensive and attractive ground cover.

distribute about the wood but so far they have not flowered. It would seem highly probable that in forty acres there was going to be a tremendous weed problem, particularly in an old wood. In point of fact it is not too bad because we try to make an intelligent use of weed-killers, and of course close-planting prevents the weeds emerging.

Another surprise, because I always thought they liked a rather more retentive soil, is how good the hydrangeas are. We have got together almost every variety we can think of and put them all in one bed. Round the outside we have planted *Agapanthus* hybrids. When I realized that I had actually collected them in running water in South Africa, it seemed somewhat surprising that they should be so happy under these very dry conditions.

Pheasants are a bit of a problem as they seem to take a liking to one or two bulbs, particularly *Lilium lankongense*; these we have to cover over with wire-netting. The odd thing about pheasants is how highly selective they are – what they take one year they will not bother with the next.

For several years we had woodcock breeding in the wood

127. A carpet of ericas beside a woodland ride.

and on one occasion drove up to three separate clutches and sat for a time watching them feed. They appeared absolutely unafraid of the car, taking no notice of it. Neither do the partridges, of which quite often there are twelve to fourteen in the wood. I suspect, although I have never been able to prove it, that they are rather fond of crocuses; however, that is a small price to pay for the privilege of their company.

We had a young man working here once, who was a very keen ornithologist, and he gave me a list of eighty-three different species of birds which he had seen in the garden.

We have now pretty well tamed a greater spotted woodpecker who, last year, brought his wife and then his family to a coconut by the house.

The making of this second garden has been a wonderful joy.

Sudbrook Cottage, Ham Common, Surrey

Beverley Nichols' Garden

Mine is the garden of a frustrated composer. Although I have written seventy books on most of the subjects under the sun my deepest emotions, since early childhood, have always been felt in terms of music. But it would need yet another book, and probably a very boring one, to explain why the music has never emerged.

How is this illustrated by the garden, on which I have now been working for over twenty years? Very clearly, if you have an ear for music and an eye for form.

Firstly, it has what may be called a 'melodic line'. This means that the main 'theme' of the garden is developed, in a series of curves, from the moment you step through the garden gate, and culminates, as in the centre section of a musical romance, in the water garden.

Secondly, and still musically, this water garden sets the key and dictates the rhythm of the whole design. One of my most obstinately held convictions is that a sheet of water in a garden is not merely a luxury but a necessity. It need not be extensive (my own is merely a circular lily-pond about twenty feet in diameter, constructed from weathered bricks) but it is essential. Water gives a garden a fourth dimension. It is like a mirror in a room. And it has a mystical quality, reflecting the sky and bringing the heavens down to earth.

Thirdly, there are no straight lines in the garden, just as there are no straight lines in Nature or in music. True, it might be argued that a Bach fugue or a Mozart sonata had 'straight lines', and that a formal garden adjoining an eighteenth-century house could be fashioned with these composers in mind. Perhaps it could, but I doubt whether the experiment would be successful.

Fourthly, just as the water, the paths and the beds dictate the melodic line, so the 'harmonization' is provided by the trees and the larger shrubs. The metaphor may be fanciful but it is also factual, as I should hope to prove to you if we were to walk round the garden together – particularly on a stormy day in October, when the wind was sweeping through the branches of the great Copper Beech.

Now for some details which distinguish my garden from the great majority of gardens in this country (by 'distinguish' I don't mean to suggest that the design is nearer to perfection – merely that it is different).

The most important distinction is seen in the fact that there are no bush roses, none of the common Hybrid Teas which appear to be so beloved by the average gardener.

Roses, of course, there are in abundance, but these are confined to the walls. But bush roses, no. When they are not flowering, which means for the greater part of the year, they are an offence to the eye, meticulously pruned and shaped in a style which bears no relation to anything in Nature. They are hospital cases, from which the eye revolts. Perhaps the most distressing are those roses in which flowers of red and yellow are born from the same root.

If I had a larger garden I should grow the old-fashioned roses beloved of Constance Spry. As it is I have to be content with one variety – the white single *R. filipes* 'Kiftsgate' which is planted all along the outer wall facing Ham Common. In July it breaks into a wave of foaming blossom, so spectacular that it draws the crowds.

One of the characteristics of my garden is that it is a 'garden for all seasons'. I could not endure a garden that was – as it were – put under dust sheets for a third of the year. Hence my passion for winter flowers. I am writing in late January, when most of the gardens in our country are lifeless. But from the window of my study I can see torrents of blossom from the Winter Cherry (*Prunus subhirtella* 'Autumnalis'). Along the outer wall there is a broad band of *Iris unguicularis* from which I have already gathered several bowls of pale blue blossom. Under the Copper Beech in the main garden there are splashes of Winter Aconite (*Eranthis hyemalis*) as bright as summer buttercups, and clusters of deep blue *Iris reticulata* mingling with the snowdrops. One of my tree heathers (*Erica arborea*) has grown to a height of ten feet, and is already trembling into blossom, and all the winter heathers (*Erica carnea*) are showing colour, undeterred by a recent snowfall. Perhaps the most spectacular shrub in the garden is a *Mahonia* 'Charity' with its long weeping clusters of palest yellow, which are serenely unaffected by the hardest frosts, as are the delicate blooms of the Cornelian Cherry (*Cornus mas*). Hellebores are to be found in abundance – not only the familiar Christmas Roses (*Helleborus niger*) but many others, varying from the greenish white *H. olympicus* to the dark crimson *H. colchicus*.

If you share my love of winter flowers and if you are too impatient to wait until daffodils 'take the winds of March with beauty', I have one variety of daffodil that makes a much earlier debut. It is called 'February Gold', and it always lives up to its name.

In spite of the wide variety of plants and trees, which give the garden a modest botanical interest, the whole thing is maintained in impeccable condition with an absolute minimum of labour. My only professional help is provided by one man who comes for three hours on Saturday mornings. There is nothing to distinguish him from the average gardening 'help' except that he happens to be a genius with a very wide botanical knowledge. He also happens to be endowed with a demonic energy which enables him to climb walls at a record speed and dig beds like a robot. No bribe would be enough to persuade me to print his name and address.

I am also lucky in having a number of ladies who must be described as 'fans'. They come along because they have read my gardening books, liked them, and decided that they wish to play a part in them. With most of them I am only acquainted – as it were – from the rear, because as soon as they step through the garden gate they bend down and start pulling up weeds.

Nor must I forget a friend who shares the cottage with me and makes himself responsible for mowing the lawns. Apart from this somewhat motley band of helpers, I have to rely on myself. And since, at my time of life, I have a limited stock of energy, and can only manage the edging and the numerous fiddly bits which nobody else will undertake, such as dead-heading the rhododendrons, the garden is, by necessity, an 'old man's garden'. But I don't think it is any the worse for that.

By an 'old man's garden' I do not mean a garden that is unimaginative or one in which there are no experiments or innovations. I mean a garden in which every possible advantage is taken of labour-saving devices. And since in these days 'labour' is scarce, lazy, capricious and absurdly expensive, every sensible person's garden must be to some extent an 'old man's garden'.

This means – to take an outstanding example – that we must all make ourselves familiar with the intelligent use of *ground cover*. A book could be written on this section alone, but I will confine myself to two examples of the ground cover which I use myself. Perhaps the most invaluable allies are to be provided by the large family of the lamiums (which have been developed from dead nettles), in particular *Lamium maculatum*, which spreads a silver carpet in spring, through which no weeds can penetrate. It is beautiful in its own right, bearing two crops of pale pink flowers which form an exquisite foil to the silver leaves. A close second is to be

128. Beverley Nichols in his garden.

found in the various periwinkles which flourish in the deepest shade, not only the blue *Vinca major* but a host of its more aristocratic relations in shades of mauve and purple.

But here we must give a word of warning. Once your lamiums and vincas have established themselves they have an alarming habit of making more and more outrageous territorial demands, even to the extent of tunnelling under concrete pavements. This is one of the few occasions when I allow the use of weed-killer in my garden, which is otherwise kept in order by blood, tears, toil and sweat. And, of course, by love, which is the most magical fertilizer of them all.

Beverley Nichols

132. The circular lily pond with the sharp yellows of pansies and tulips.

129 and 130 (*left above and centre*). The great Copper Beech is a central feature of this attractive small garden. Yellow azaleas and *Euphorbia* are planted beneath it.
131 (*left below*). A mixed planting in spring. A ten-foot *Erica arborea* blends with a *Philadelphus*.

133. A splendid clump of *Lilium regale* in front of golden robinia.

134. A well-placed group of *Iris sibirica*.

Acacia, Lunedale Road, Dibden Purlieu, Hampshire

Fred Nutbeam's Garden

It was at the end of June 1974 that we received a call from our elder daughter in Brussels asking us: 'Isn't it nearly time you started to look for a home to retire to?' At that time we had not seriously contemplated retirement. We were not even sure where we wished to settle, only to agree that it would be in the south, and not too far from the sea.

During the next few months we looked over dozens of properties. Most of those we liked were either in the wrong place, the garden was too small, or the soil was not suitable for my needs. We did not require a large house and wanted a garden only large enough to be interesting without tying up every minute of our leisure time. We chose our present home at the end of October in a village in the New Forest, next to the one I had left forty-five years before as a young journeyman gardener to work on large estates in various parts of the country. Since leaving the Royal Navy in 1945 I have had charge of two very large gardens, equally interesting yet so vastly different in every way, one an isolated castle in Wales, the other a garden of over forty acres in the heart of London.

I now found myself with a plot of land some 220 by 40 feet, almost bare apart from a pear and a couple of apple trees of unknown origin, a fence on one side, and a hedge running down the other. Half the garden was lush grass, the rest a neglected vegetable plot. How I would have loved some old walls. Having spent a weekend 'walking the ground', the only advantages we found were a couple of birches *Betula pendula* and a *Pinus sylvestris* over the boundary on the southern and weather side.

Back in London I sat down and made a plan (my garden had to be productive as well as ornamental), splitting the area into three, one for pleasure, one for orchard fruit, the other for soft fruit and vegetables, knowing also that the time I would be able to spend on it for the next three years would be about one weekend in three.

The first task was to get it into workable shape. Three applications of chemicals were enough to clear the rough and overgrown area – that, and a very helpful young brother-in-law who rough-dug and cleared all the buried debris. Meanwhile the grass had been rotoscythed several times, well raked and swept; the garden was now in reasonable condition to think about preparing to plant. Mid-January saw the delivery of the fruit trees I had ordered and, as the weather was kind, I decided to plant the orchard section, twenty-four feet by forty, straight into grass and immediately behind where the main shrub border would be sited, seven varieties of apples and one pear 'Conference', all on dwarfing stock. The border was then marked out to sweep away in a wide arc moving from right to left. Knowing only too well the necessity of soil preparation for permanent planting, the turf was removed, and was used to lay a grass path through the middle of the vegetable garden, the remainder being stacked for future use as potting soil. The border was then trenched, using a liberal dressing of farmyard manure to which was added bales of moss peat and bags of spent hops.

Planting began at the end of March, using conifers to create a background interest and to blind out unsightly sheds etc.: *Chamaecyparis lawsoniana* 'Ellwoodii', 'Fletcheri', 'Pottenii' and × *Cupressocyparis leylandii* 'Castlewellan'; a collection of camellias using *C. japonica* 'Adolphe Audusson', 'Apollo', 'Madame Victor de Bisschop', 'Lady Vansittart', 'Mathotiana Rosea'; *C. williamsii* 'Donation', 'Citation', 'Golden Spangles', 'Elizabeth Rothschild'; *C. reticulata* 'Butterfly Wings', *C. saluenensis*; Rhododendrons 'Fred Wynniatt', *davidsonianum, moupinense*, Cilpinense, 'Blue Tit', Praecox and 'Bric-à-Brac'; several varieties of *Pieris* including *P.* 'Forest Flame', *P. forrestii, P. japonica, P. japonica* 'Variegata', a *Kalmia latifolia*, and the whole side of the border facing the cottage a frontal planting of evergreen azaleas using such varieties as 'Amoenum', 'Addy Wery', 'Blaauw's Pink', 'Palestrina', 'Hinomayo', 'Rosebud' and many others; these were then interplanted at the back end of the year with *Crocus chrysanthus* to give early spring colour.

To break the stark line of the cottage I used Virginia Creeper *Parthenocissus quinquefolia* and *Chaenomeles speciosa* 'Moerloesii', and to mask a long brick outhouse a fan-trained peach 'Peregrine', a Strawberry Vine *Vitis vinifera* 'Fragola' and *Hydrangea petiolaris*.

The only other plantings for that year were a mulberry *Morus nigra* and *Salix matsudana* 'Tortuosa' to break up the line of the wall in the front of the house. I persuaded my neighbour to allow me to plant *Clematis montana rubens* over a shed at the foot of his garden for our mutual benefit, and finally to prepare and plant a bed of asparagus, a gift of fifty two-year-old crowns from Mr Fred Potter of Suttons.

That year our infrequent visits were to water, mow and work the ground left fallow. By the end of the year we had underplanted the orchard area with narcissi and crocus, while other small bulbs were introduced into the lawn and through shrubs etc.

The next to receive attention was the soft fruit – four bushes each of four varieties of blackcurrants, two rows of raspberries, thornless loganberries and blackberries put on fences, and a row of struck gooseberry cuttings 'Leveller' ready to be trained as cordons. All, we hoped, would be established by the time we retired.

The border that had lain fallow was prepared for spring planting. *Eucalyptus gunnii* was put in to eventually take the

135. A view looking towards the rear of the garden through a *Clematis*-covered hoop. A group of *Chaemaecyparis* is used to give background interest.

136. A single pink camellia, *C. saluenensis*, demonstrates the remarkable vigour of all the plants in this garden.

137. A cascade of *Rhododendron moupinense* with *Verbena rigida* in early spring.

place of the birches that were showing signs of deterioration and to give winter colour. The shrubs included: *Pieris* 'Blush' and *P. forrestii* 'Jermyns' (a gift from Mr Hillier), deciduous azaleas, *Choisya ternata*, *Pittosporum tenuifolium* 'Silver Queen', *Cistus* 'Sunset', *Elaeagnus pungens* 'Dicksonii', *Ilex aquifolium* 'Ferox Aurea', *Genista hispanica*, ten varieties of ericas, several varieties of hostas and many others.

This (the year of the drought) was the end of my planting for over two years. Unfortunately the rest of 1977 and part of the following year were spent in and out of hospital for a series of operations and I only saw the garden five times until I took a late retirement at the end of June 1978, with a warning from the specialist 'no more lifting or bending'. This was a bit of a blow to one who had spent a lifetime doing both. However, it is surprising how you learn to improvise.

Before the end of that year the greenhouse I had purchased and stored had been erected by a kind friend in the glasshouse world. Life began once more to have a purpose. A bed was prepared and planted with roses (a gift from our friends Cockers of Aberdeen), cages were built over the fruit in the vegetable garden.

The border in front of the cottage which was partly furnished was enlarged and shrubs added to give colour. These included: several of the Blue *Rhododendron augustinii* type, *Ceanothus* 'Cascade', and plants to give summer and autumn colour such as *Euonymus fortunei* 'Emerald 'n' Gold', *Hypericum × inodorum*, *Spiraea × bumalda* 'Gold Flame', *Leucothoe fontanesiana* 'Rainbow', *Fothergilla monticola*, *Berberis thunbergii* 'Rose Glow'.

The fence down one side of the house was planted with climbing roses which included 'Altissimo', 'Dreaming Spires', 'Handel' and 'Malaga'.

Many other plants, trees, shrubs and conifers have found their way into the garden in the past two years, and the patio has been furnished with vases. The greenhouse, which now has a propagator installed, is the means of raising all the soft and hardwood cuttings and bedding plants required, and also houses a small collection of orchids.

Gardening and naturalist friends knowing my passion for collecting forecast that I would soon run out of garden. Fortunately one can always overflow into those of neighbours and friends who appreciate plants of interest and perhaps bring to them some of the pleasure that my garden has brought to us in our retirement.

Fred Wuthin

138. Drifts of daffodils and early-flowering camellias make a colourful show in spring.

139. An island bed with pansies and campanulas surrounding a pink Hybrid Tea rose 'Silver Jubilee' and the Floribunda 'Anne Cocker'.

140. This garden, planted since 1975, is now growing to maturity. *Pieris formosa forrestii* 'Wakehurst' in the background, azaleas 'Orange Triumph', 'Vuyk's Scarlet' and 'Rosebud' bloom in the spring.

The Old Rectory, Naunton, Gloucestershire

Nicholas Ridley's Garden

When I bought the Old Rectory in 1959 the house was derelict and the garden was an abandoned area of flat land. It was ringed with high Cotswold stone walls and old yew trees, provided, no doubt, for the greater privacy, dignity and solemnity of a series of incumbents. One of these was a Reverend Litton. He was a close friend of Canon Charles Dodgson, who visited for his holidays from Oxford, and is alleged to have written *Alice in Wonderland* at Naunton. Our croquet lawn was said to be the famous one. I have since heard of half a dozen croquet lawns which also claim this distinction; but we keep the croquet lawn just in case!

It was obvious from the start that the potential for making a garden was the River Windrush, which flowed along one side of the rectangular area of nettles and elders I had acquired, again behind a high stone wall. Ten miles higher up the Cotswolds, where this lovely river rises, the rock is porous, and the rain water is stored in it. Neither heavy downpour nor drought affects the water level very much. Thus there is enough water in periods of drought to keep water plants happy: and flooding is exceptional. I determined from the beginning to divert some of the river's flow through the garden. One of the first tasks was to demolish the wall that separated the river from the garden, so that we could see it!

As the whole area is less than one acre, I decided to make it into a series of 'rooms' divided up by high stone walls, and by the high Copper Beech hedge which I planted on my arrival. This gives a feeling of intimacy. It allows interesting vistas from one 'room' to another, and also gives the visitor surprises. We have three 'rooms' which are water gardens – first, the formal, symmetrical one complementing the Georgian side of the house. There is a sunken round pond, flanked with large paving stones and steps up to herbaceous borders on each side. From it, under a classical bridge, runs

a formal canal. It is here that we keep about fifty rainbow trout, for gastronomic reasons as well as for the joy of seeing them jumping for the May fly.

The second water garden is a wild one, with four streams from the river running through it. They flow abandonedly under bridges and round islands, finally mingling again to rejoin the river. The third is a sunken garden, half formal, half informal. It is flanked by a low stone wall incorporating stone carved signs of the Zodiac: we call it the Zodiac garden.

None of them are finished – but nothing ever is, nor should be in a garden. I have made them virtually single handed over twenty-two years of weekends, and need at least as long again to complete my work.

At first I was more interested in building than in plants. I set out constructing walls, bridges, paths, water-courses, aqueducts and pillars, all out of the local stone, which lay about in heaps. As I ran out first of stone and then of space, I began to get more interested in what to grow in the garden, and exchanged my mason's mallet and chisels for my trowel and fork.

I got interested in different families of plants in turn. By studying and trying all the varieties of a family and how to grow them and propagate them, I could acquire a small parcel of professionalism in my sea of general ignorance. I could then move onto the next family. Lime-haters – azaleas, camellias, magnolias and rhododendrons – were discarded in our limy soil; but there are still many, many families (lime-tolerant, no doubt) which remain unlearned.

My first love was primulas and all three water gardens are crammed with every sort. They thrive on the wet edges and islands of the water-courses, and grow best with masses of leaf mould forked into the soil in autumn. We grow them both from seed and by splitting them in autumn. They provide colour and interest from March right through the

141 (*above*). The Georgian façade of the Old Rectory overlooks a formal water garden. The narrow Lutyens-like canal, flanked with scented June-flowering iris, is backed by decorative, grey-leafed artichokes – an unusual combination. The now well-established Copper Beech hedge was planted in 1959.

142 (*below*). Nicholas Ridley's imagination and architectural sense, his feeling for stone and expertise with mason's mallet have given this formal garden an individuality of its own, all in perfect proportion and enhanced by his choice of plants. The brick pillars actually carry water pipes in the Roman style – most useful for summer irrigation.

summer until October. First come *P. rosea* in thick pads of violent carmine, follow by *P. denticulata* (the Drumstick Primula) in shades of blue, mauve and white. Then comes the beautiful blue *P. sonchifolia*, and next the tiny wax-white *P. involucrata*. In May the candelabra primulas begin to flower: *P. pulverulenta, P. aurantiaca, P. beesiana, P. burmanica*, etc.; tall farinose stems carry whorls of brilliant flowers. Many have hybridized and we have them in every colour from yellow through red to purple. *P. nutans* and *P. vialii* (the Red Hot Poker Primula), *P. secundiflora* and *P. poissonii*, and many others take over in July, with *P. florindae* (the Giant Cowslip) lingering on into autumn, red, yellow and gold.

Next I collected and learned about willows, which also thrive in our water garden and give welcome shade to the primulas. When they get too big, I either pollard them or cut them down completely and start them again. They are the easiest of plants to reproduce; simply stick a cutting into the ground any time during winter. We have about forty different varieties growing, from the tiniest to great trees. They provide all-year-round interest: the bark in midwinter, the catkins in early spring and the green leaves in summer. I recommend the white bark of *S. pendulifolia* and the claret-coloured catkins of *S. 'Melanostachys'*; also the wonderful woolly leaves and catkins of *S. lanata*, of which we have three

143. Willows combine well with primulas, giving all-year-round interest.

varieties. They make ideal house decorations in February and March. We also grow yellow and white lysichitums in the wild garden, and numerous varieties of *Caltha*, and water irises, including *I. kaemferi*, with its magnificent royal purple flowers.

On the banks of the water gardens above the primulas we have planted campanulas, geraniums, *Dianthus*, saxifrage, *Vinca* and *Pulmonaria* providing a mass of summer colour.

Another family which we cultivated was *Iris*. These grow erect and formal either side of the canal. During the first two weeks of June they provide a spectacular display. They are all tall bearded irises with scented flowers in every shade. Behind them are globe artichokes which provide superb summer eating and have wonderfully decorative leaves.

The two small herbaceous borders on either side of the formal water garden are filled with pastel-shaded flowering plants, delphiniums, *Phlox*, peonies, *Nepeta* and roses, with some darker varieties to add depth. We have also planted many lilies, which fill the garden with their magical scent in July and August.

Next we explored *Clematis*: they thrive in our limy soil, and look very effective against the stone walls. We grow them up every wall, pillar and tree that we can. *C. florida 'Sieboldii'*, with its large saucer-shaped white flowers and purple staminodes, is one of our favourites, and also the evergreen *C. armandii* which flowers bravely in early spring, sometimes amid the snow, and has delicate light pink flowers. The yellow lantern-shaped flower of *C. tangutica* is another we love. It is followed by a silvery seed head, like a tiny powder puff.

We are always planning new 'rooms'. Recently we have started to develop the area of the famous croquet lawn. It must stay for ever, but the untidy yew trees which surround it are to be tidied up and filled with *Clematis* and climbing roses, including the celebrated *R. filipes 'Kiftsgate'*, which grows like Jack's famous beanstalk. In addition, there will be criss-crossing avenues of willows; and groups of trees in between with long grass and spring bulbs. There will be a 'nuttery' – but we can only think of four English edible nuts – the almond, the hazel, the Sweet Chestnut and the walnut.

The garden gives us endless pleasure at every season, despite its small size. The contrast between the willows covered in catkins against a background of snow in midwinter, and the midsummer riot of colour from the primulas, irises and a host of other plants, is a constant joy. Moreover it lasts a lifetime. There is never a dull moment – only work to do and improvements to make.

144. The sunken garden in winter is dominated by the stone carved signs of the Zodiac. In spring and summer the emphasis turns to the beauty of the Candelabra primulas.

145. Stonework has been introduced into the wild garden as a contrast to twisted willows.

146. In the wild water garden four streams have been diverted from the River Windrush. Here there are small islands where interesting opportunities have been created for groups of moisture-loving plants.

Magnolia House, Yoxford, Suffolk

Mark Rumary's Garden

I shall never forget my excitement when I first saw this garden twenty years ago. It is hidden from the village street by the small eighteenth-century house so I was quite unprepared for a completely walled garden which, instead of being the ubiquitous rectangle, had unexpected curves and projections, and best of all disappeared out of sight round a corner, providing that element of mystery so desirable in a garden. In one corner stood a Victorian stable with a pigeon loft, while at right angles to the opposite wall was a high brick arch, all that remained of the earlier stable yard.

Walls can cause turbulence, but I saw that the garden would be very sheltered, for beyond the south-west boundary grew a belt of magnificent elms. My heart rejoiced, for the greatest drawback to gardening in East Anglia, apart from the lowest rainfall in the country, is the cold drying winds.

Ignoring the narrow crumbling brick paths, the dangerous tilt of one of the walls and the diseased old fruit trees standing in a sea of ground elder, I saw instead an emerald lawn, surrounded by exciting plants from warmer climes, luxuriating in the shelter of the high walls. It did not take me long to find out, however, that the walls and elms not only cast long shadows but also created a frost pocket.

The second problem I had to contend with was the poor sandy soil, 'the soil with the least back-ache and the most heart-ache'. This, combined with the low rainfall and the shadows, produced areas with that most difficult of conditions, dry shade. Farmyard manure, peat and, above all, compost have improved the moisture-holding properties of the soil, but even so there are usually one or two periods each year when I am forced to water.

Of the trees and shrubs that were here when we came, only ten were kept, the most important being an ancient mulberry, three Irish Yews, a *Juniperus chinensis* which has made an open tree forty feet tall, and close to it and nearly two-thirds of its height, the biggest *Philadelphus* I have ever seen. There were no magnolias; the deeds however showed that the property had been Magnolia House throughout the nineteenth century so several kinds were given prominent positions in the new planting. Of these *M. kobus loebneri* is now a small tree and looks like a cloud of white butterflies every April.

Having taken account of the climate, soil and existing features, I could begin to plan. My principal aims were: style and materials in sympathy with the old house; the ability to change and augment a wide range of plants without losing the overall lines of the design; to be able to enjoy the pleasures of active gardening without feeling it was a burden; above all, in Gertrude Jekyll's words, 'to paint a year long succession of living pictures'.

The garden covers only one-third of an acre but I knew it could be made to appear larger and more interesting if subdivided into a number of smaller enclosures. Its unusual shape made this easy. I linked the stable to the arch with a yew hedge and cut off the vegetable garden, which occupied the area hidden from the house, with a mixture of beech and holly. This was an unwise choice. The holly prickles made weeding so unpleasant that I soon changed them for *Osmanthus heterophyllus*. I wish I had also changed the beech, because the falling leaves add an unwelcome touch of autumn to spring. More successful have been pleached hornbeams, planted to gain extra height above the six-foot-high roadside wall, and which have successfully reduced the noise of traffic.

While each area is self-contained, I made sure that openings were so placed that the longest possible views were kept, and that there was something at the end of each vista on which the eye could rest. My intention was to give each area its own character, both in its proportions and choice of plants. The largest part of the garden has only narrow borders, so that the lawn, which has a curving outline in contrast to the straight lines elsewhere, could be as large as possible. The small garden through the arch was given heavier planting and less open space, while only white flowers were allowed.

Having settled on the main lines of the plan, I could turn my attention to the planting. I think I should here explain that while I have designed many gardens for other people, this was the first I had made for myself, and much more difficult it proved to be, for it is so easy to be carried away by the desire to grow too many sorts of plants in too small a space, or to use plants of the wrong character. It is far easier to be firm with other people than with oneself! Over the years there has been a constant battle between designer and plantsman, for while by training I belong to the former, by instinct I am of the latter. It is a Dr Jekyll and Mr Hyde situation, or in this case Miss Jekyll and Mr Hyde! In the early stages Jekyll had the upper hand; form, texture and colour, not only of flowers but of foliage, were carefully considered; plants suited to an enclosed, rather formal garden, such as Japanese Cherries, hybrid lilacs, deutzias, irises and peonies, were selected. Genera which need a more natural or informal setting, including heathers, brooms and rhododendrons, were eschewed, but Hyde would keep popping up, and he still does. As Landscape Director of Notcutts, one of the country's leading nurseries, I am constantly meeting plants which I want to try. Sometimes I spend hours wandering about with a plant, trying to find a home where it will not spoil the design. At the same time I cannot bear to part with old friends.

It was not long before the vegetables were banished to a scrap of ground beside the toolshed. My excuse was that they took up too much of my time. Certainly the only help I have is with lawnmowing and I can only work in the garden at weekends, but the real reason is that I wanted space in which to re-create something of the character of the courtyard gardens of southern Spain. A raised pool was built in the shape often seen in classical Mediterranean gardens, and doubtless of Moorish origin. The advantage of a raised pool is that it allows one to sit on the edge and enjoy the fountain, water-lilies and the flashing colours of the carp and goldfish at close quarters. The Mediterranean feeling is underlined with tubs of oleanders, daturas and agaves which spend the winter in the small conservatory.

The accent in the beds around the pool is on colour. In early spring the pink rosettes of *Prunus triloba* 'Multiplex' are seen above a drift of *Chionoscilla allenii*, a rarely seen cross between *Chionodoxa luciliae* and *Scilla bifolia*, the present of a generous neighbour whose family have treasured it for years. A similar colour combination is repeated later with *Kolkwitzia* 'Pink Cloud' in front of a soft blue *Ceanothus* 'Cascade'. Midsummer brings the old striped roses with mauve campanulas and purple alliums. For late summer and autumn there are jasmine and heliotrope which with buddleias and *Sedum* attract masses of butterflies who seem to appreciate the shelter.

147. The small garden where only white flowers are allowed.

148. A cleverly arranged path of contrasting bricks and cobbles curves out of sight behind a high brick wall.

149. An old lead pump is used to provide moisture in a raised bed.

Alas, some of that shelter has now gone, for last summer most of the elms succumbed to Dutch elm disease. The superb backdrop which they provided is no more, but there will be the great advantage that the garden will be sunlit till late in the afternoon.

One of the previous advantages which I hope we shall not have lost is that, in a garden in which the air is largely still, scents are not so quickly dispersed. Certain plants, such as *Daphne odora* 'Aureomarginata', Sweet Brier (*Rosa eglanteria*) and honeysuckle, actually give off their scent into currents of warm air. These bursts of scent are not continuous and thus are tantalizingly elusive and unexpected. Sometimes they can be carried a considerable distance from the plant itself. The scent of Winter Sweet (*Chimonanthus praecox*) and Night-Scented Stock (*Matthiola bicornis*) can drift for many yards as can the less attractive smell of expanding Crown Imperials (*Fritillaria imperialis*).

The time I enjoy the garden most of all is in the evening after it has been open to the public, realizing that I can now relax for a week or two. Remembering the compliments which kind people have paid, I think that it is perhaps *not* necessary to pull everything out and start all over again!

Mark Rumary

150. Rare multicoloured carp swim in a Moorish raised pool in this very Mediterranean corner of the garden where in summer there are many tubs of exotic plants.

151. An arch in the beech hedge leads to another compartment of the garden. The blue *Agapanthus* stand out in the foreground.

152. Looking away from the raised pool, an antique urn closes the view. Exceptionally well-chosen plants border the path, including *Allium christophii* in the foreground.

The Dower House, Boughton House, Kettering, Northamptonshire

Sir David Scott's Garden

The Dower House of Boughton House, where I now live, was lent to my parents for six months in 1903. My father died there in 1911, my mother in 1942 and I came back there with my first wife in 1947! My parents' garden consisted of a small piece of ground against the house, with the ritual roses of the day (some are still flourishing – a 'Leonie Lamesch' is useful for testing visitors' knowledge), an equally ritual tiny herbaceous border and a fair-sized vegetable garden.

To a shrub addict like myself who was determined to have a shrub garden this amount of space was quite insufficient, so I had to look about for somewhere to expand. I eventually realized, though reluctantly, that the only piece of ground that was possible (and which providentially adjoined the vegetable garden) was a square of some 100 yards by 100 (about two acres) which used to form part of the park of Boughton House and had for generations been grazed by fallow deer, but which, when the deer were fenced off about 1907, had speedily reverted to the wild. It would have been difficult to find a more unpromising and daunting site for making a shrub or any other kind of garden. Dominated by two colossal elms and several ancient stag-headed lime trees, it was no more than a vast thicket. It sloped facing north, got little winter sun and the underlying soil was an inhospitable Northamptonshire clay with, I found, a pH of 7.5, in places even 8. But there was nowhere else for me to expand, so I had to make the best of it.

The elms and limes were soon cut down and removed by professionals, but the rest my wife and I valiantly (we were both over sixty) decided to tackle ourselves. We also decided to ask no outside advice, and I am eternally glad that we did not, for I am sure that I could never look on a garden designed by someone else with the affectionate and indulgent eye with which I now survey a garden planned, dug and planted entirely by myself.

I say 'planned' but I should rather say 'created', for I never had a plan or design of any sort in my head: no thought of a vista or an axis – indeed, I am not quite sure that I know even now what the much used word 'axis' denotes gardenwise. I just started off clearing a track through the middle of the jungle, dodging the worst tree stumps, with my wife jabbing in bits of grass here and there which surprisingly soon joined up to make a rough mowable grass path; and as I progressed I planted. I realized now that at the back of my mind – a plantsman's mind – was nothing more than a desire to grow a lot of different shrubs and trees and woodland plants, not to make a regular garden.

So I kept nibbling away, the mattock and billhook my main tools, and every now and then tributary paths demanded creation and from time to time island beds, where a grouping of shrubs seemed to require them. And thus, bit by bit, as the years went by – it was a slow process – the whole jungle got tamed, except for a corner left to conceal things like bonfires and leaf and compost heaps and a strip where two ancient but sacrosanct limes made gardening near them imprudent.

Just as I had no plan, so, except for a block of willows and dogwood with coloured barks, I devised no plant associations. The welfare of the trees and shrubs was always the overriding consideration, so that, not surprisingly, the final result was more a home for plants than a garden. But in spite of the haphazardness of it all the general effect is not, in my eyes anyhow, unpleasing. A garden should have variety and surprises. I like to think mine has both. There is a multiplicity of shrubs and trees and plants, resulting in all kinds of shapes and colours, and the blocks of shrubs with the winding grass paths and occasional open spaces make for surprises. It is not easy to say into what category of garden it falls, but it has character, if a somewhat undefinable one. Though I have, as I say, disregarded the problem of plant association, my experience is that if you eschew, as I do, the difficult orange hues (I must admit that I grow *Buddleja globosa*), colours seldom clash – or is it that an owner often turns a blind eye?

Naturally I have made many mistakes and naturally I have not always learned from them. It took me a long time to resist the temptation of putting in too old a plant. Some of these O.A.P.s. have hardly moved in thirty years and I am even now not nearly ruthless enough about throwing out bad doers or plants, bought perhaps from a catalogue description or just because they were rare (B.I.O.s, I call the latter – Botanical Interest Only), which have turned out disappointingly. I hardly know why I preserve these ancient monuments which still stand here and there, watching me apprehensively whenever I pass by. And I have too often made the mistake of planting too close together: and oh! the anguish of having to decide later on which of two jostling neighbours to sacrifice. And then there are the grass paths: I have erred, in places, when making them, over their width. The error is irremediable if you make them too narrow; six feet is not too wide for a main path for two people walking abreast in a garden like mine. It saves time and effort when mowing the paths if you have tailored them to the width of the cutters of your machine.

Again, I have sometimes demanded too much of the lime-haters, but it was cruel of me to ask *Lindera obtusiloba* to survive and I should have taken more warning than I did when twice a *Desfontainea spinosa* has expired in an effort to produce its improbable but lovely flowers. Nonetheless I would always recommend venturesomeness to a gardener. I was assured, for instance, that *Hamamelis* would not 'do' with me, whereas they seem quite reasonably happy here and *H.* 'Pallida' never fails to enchant me every winter.

My first wife died in 1965 and five years later I married Valerie Finnis. Not surprisingly with her advent the whole garden was transfigured. The patch by the house was embellished with interesting and beautiful plants (the two things do not by any means always go together!) and an array of old stone troughs. The vegetable garden, while still, thanks to intensive cultivation, producing enough for the house, spawned 200 yards of raised beds, seventy yards of them made up with imported acid soil, making homes for thousands of small hardy plants; an adjacent yard, once used by stonemasons, where for many years I kept bees and, as a boy, hawks, was peppered with frames and edged with more raised beds; two small greenhouses and an alpine house

made their appearance and there was a spectacular increase in the number and interestingness of the island beds in the area which I had reclaimed and which is still, in spite of this face-lift, carefully referred to as 'David's garden'.

Although so much has been done since 1970 to increase the productivity and number of ingredients in the whole garden, we still contrive, sometimes to my mild astonishment, to manage it all with no more help than a man – but *what* a man! – once a week to mow and do any really heavy work, and occasional kind friends. But we could never cope without rubber knee-pads (we live in them, and the whole garden, except for the vegetables and fruit, is hand-weeded for the sake of chance seedlings), a first-class mower and a

153. Sir David Scott, now in his nineties, values a turn with the scythe. Here, he is trimming the grass around a treasured *Rubus* Tridel.

154. A trough beside the porch door. In this garden the alpines are chiefly grown in raised beds by his wife, Valerie Finnis, but this stone sink is cherished by Sir David himself.

155. A winter scene where the coloured stems of carefully pollarded willows make a delicate tracery.

156. An island bed in April where blue and lime green predominate. *Euphorbia polychroma* and *Helleborus* 'Boughton Beauty' hybrid have developed into handsome clumps.

157. A group of shade-loving plants. The sculptural leaves of *Rheum palmatum* provide a pleasing and sharp contrast to the *Dicentra*'s delicate greenery.

158. More formal beds of hardy perennials, in a striking variety of shapes and colours, border a grassy path.

Flymo, as well as a battery spintrim for the grass edges (if you want to impress visitors, as every gardener does, keep your edges trimmed), white paint on the wooden part of all our tools: 'where did you leave the rubber rake?' 'Over there, can't you see?' – and, to save lengthy domestic explanations, names for all the beds (some fifty-five island beds in 'David's garden' alone): 'Where will you be working this afternoon?' 'In the Barrett border.'

I sometimes wonder, as I perambulate my garden on a smiling summer's day and ruminate on the past, how on earth I managed to get it all like this and what did I and do I most enjoy about it all. I think the answer to the first question is simply 'it took an awfully long time!', but to the second I find it much more difficult to reply. Was it and is it still something as mundane as hand-weeding? I get such enormous satisfaction from actions like drawing out unbroken a long strand of twitch or ground elder. Or is it planting, with all its exciting preliminaries? Or potting up my own well-rooted cuttings? And what about the first *Hepatica* or aconite, or smelling the Winter Heliotrope (*Petasites fragrans*, a dangerous weed in the wrong place!) or one of the exquisite winter honeysuckles (*Lonicera purpusii* or *L. fragrantissima*, too often shy flowers)? Or just sitting on a seat – there are fourteen in my little garden; not one too many – revelling in the coloured stems of the willows on a winter's morning, white, yellow and red or peering at the buttercup yellow of a lowly celandine? I could go on indefinitely and still not make up my mind. No, I think the answer to my second question can only be just the one word 'gardening', a pursuit which has the inestimable merit, especially for the not so young, of always offering something to look forward to as well as always having an exhilarating variety of jobs to do.

Marwood Hill, Barnstaple, North Devon

Dr James Smart's Garden

It was not until 1949 when I moved to Devonshire and bought an early Georgian house that I could really get my teeth into gardening.

The house was typically Georgian in as much as the garden was at a distance from the house but, unfortunately, there were no trees or plants of any merit in it at all. There was a triple row of bamboos, a fuchsia hedge, but no decorative trees of any kind with the exception of a very fine plant of *Rhododendron* Nobleanum, which was practically the reason why I bought the house. I was soon to be deflated as the year after I moved in this died of honey fungus.

Thus the garden was a major challenge. The whole garden is on a slope going down into a valley and, while sloping land adds considerably to the interest of a garden, it also adds very much to the work entailed. My assistance at this time was from an ex-sailor who had seen service in the Boxer rebellion and whose chief joy in life was growing outsize leeks. It was not until myxomatosis had taken its toll and I bought in more land to the south across a small valley with a stream in it that I could really start any serious planning. Practically any good shrub or tree in the garden therefore dates from 1960 or later. This small stream has never dried up even in the severe drought of 1976 and it was a natural development to dam it off and thus produce two small lakes, one of which has an island.

The soil on the far side of the lakes is acid, as I first discovered on planting some large red hydrangeas which I had moved from the main garden into the new piece of land. The following year they were covered in deep blue flowers; large plants moved in a big ball of soil had changed colour within twelve months, thus demonstrating the litmus-paper quality of this shrub, which justifies the Devonshire name for hydrangeas of 'Changeables'.

My object was to make the trees and shrubs grow happily and fairly haphazard planting has not interfered with later attention to some degree of landscaping. This was planned to fit in with the modern split-level house which I built in the garden and moved into in 1973. The trees are planted in grass and, as I soon discovered, it is essential for good growth to keep the grass under control in a wide area around the plant. This has been done ever since with the help of Paraquat. Drifts of bulbs are planted amongst the trees and are kept in good condition by applying a general fertilizer every second year. *Cyclamen hederifolium*, pink and white forms, and *C. coum* have gradually been increased by seed and grow around the bases of most of the trees. This has led to some very pretty colour combinations, as when the autumn colour of *Prunus sargentii* leaves form a carpet through which the pink and white cyclamen push their heads.

The walled garden is now practically filled with glass structures, for in addition to the camellia house there is a propagating house with mist benches and internal frames for grafting, and another greenhouse given over entirely to Australian plants. I have been visiting that continent for a number of years and have become fascinated with the flora; many of them will grow outside but I keep them in until I have propagated them. I believe that many more of the *Eucalyptus* family could be grown in this country and correas, several callistemons, *Melaleuca squarrosa, Prostanthera cuneata* all do well outside. I have the purple and white berried billardieras fruiting freely on the wall and have now raised from seed a reputedly pink one from Tasmania. The excess of plants propagated over and above my requirements are sold to visitors to the garden, which is open to the public throughout the year. They are put on display in the walled garden and payment is through an honesty box. In this way quite a lot of expenses of the garden are paid and it has been possible to keep the majority of the plants labelled, a service which I find much appreciated.

Malcolm Pharoah, who came to work here nine years ago, has played an enormous part in developing the garden. We have together put in a heather garden and a large bog garden, turned a small disused quarry into an alpine garden, and planted a thyme lawn through which grow miniature bulbs collected in Portugal. White Arum Lilies thrive in the water at the margin of the lakes but must have their crowns below the level of the water to avoid freezing. Grown in this way the flowers are as fine as you will get in a greenhouse, and the moorhens, by turning the leaves over, find them an excellent place to build their nests. A new development this year is a bed of hebes which with the parahebes and Australian species should prove interesting in the latter part of the year. They range from the large shrubby types with quite spectacular flowers, some of them scented, down to the dwarf conifer appearance of *H. cupressoides* or *H. epacridea*.

It appears to be fashionable these days to despise Hybrid Tea roses in favour of the species; however I am unashamedly fond of them and have them in a formal rose garden with each bed containing just one variety. One of my favourites is 'Peer Gynt', a neat compact grower, and although I have always been taught not to have ground cover in rose beds I find that *Malvastrum lateritium* looks extremely well under 'Peer Gynt', dies to the ground in the winter and prevents weeds in the summer.

Around the walled garden I have planted many tender plants intermingled and in competition with various *Ceanothus*, Australian plants, *Fremontodendron* 'California Glory', *Stachyurus praecox*, *Feijoa sellowiana*, and sundry Pittosporums competing with *Clematis*, particularly the

159. The small stream has been dammed to make two lakes in the bottom of the valley, which has greatly enhanced the landscape.

160. Looking across one of the lakes at a fine display of *Prunus* 'Shirotae' (Mount Fuji).

161. Primulas, astilbes and other spring-flowering plants line a stream in the bog garden.

small-flowered *C. viticella* and *C. texensis* hybrids; these are trained fan-shaped to occupy a maximum area. *Eccremocarpus scaber*, the pink form, looks well through and above *Ceanothus papillosus* and *C. cyaneus*. *Acacia pravissima* further along the wall flowers freely and is the hardiest of the family. Callistemons and leptospermums also take their place.

I cannot agree with a certain body of opinion in this country which will not accept *Eucalyptus* as part of the garden scene. A project that I have at the moment is to grow a small area of different species of *Eucalyptus* alongside a similar area of different betulas for contrasting bark values.

I am fond of *Abies koreana*, bearing its purple cones in profusion from quite an early age and well set off against the silver-backed needles. It is slow-growing and keeps compact. Another tree in the same area is *Pinus sylvestris* 'Aurea', the Golden Scots Pine, which is slower-growing than the type and assumes a golden mantle in the winter.

I use a medium-coarse pine bark extensively to cut down on the weeding in any exposed earth; this also provides a good medium for the coarser seeds such as *Pittosporum*. I have found Roundup invaluable for control of Couch Grass and sorrel in these areas and Clovercide Extra is used around the trees for keeping down Milfoil as well as clover etc.

Texture of foliage and bark in all its forms is of increasing interest to me and although I enjoy the garden enormously when the daffodils are at their best, when the rhododendron are in full flower, and when the bog garden is a mass of colour with the candlelabra primulas, astilbes, *Iris kaempferi* etc., nevertheless I derive a more subtle enjoyment from the stems of *Prunus serrula, P. maackii, Acer griseum, Cupressus guadalupensis, Arbutus menziesii* and all the betulas. One of my favourite plants in the garden is *Eucalyptus niphophila*, the Snow Gum, which I see across the valley from my house with its white trunk and perpetually twinkling leaves as they move with the slightest breeze.

I think that one has to assume as a gardener that one will live forever and going on this principle I have only just planted a grafted plant of *Magnolia campbellii*. All right, I may never see it bloom, but as long as it grows healthily I continue to enjoy it and others will reap the joy of the flowers in later years.

Gardening has always been an enormous pleasure to me as a pastime and as a hobby but I have an increasing suspicion that it is also a disease, at times infectious, and certainly, as far as I am concerned, quite incurable.

James A. Smart

162. *Cyclamen hederifolium.*

163. *Pulsatilla vulgaris* with dark red flowers.

164. A purple-hued variation of *Pulsatilla vulgaris.*

York Gate, Adel, West Yorkshire

Robin Spencer's Garden

In 1977 I changed, somewhat with tongue in cheek, our entry in the yellow book *Gardens Open to the Public in England and Wales* to read:

An owner-made and maintained garden of particular interest to the plantsman, containing orchard with pool, an arbour, miniature pinetum, dell with stream, a Folly, nut walk, peony bed, iris borders, fern border, herb garden, summerhouse, alley, white and silver garden, two vegetable gardens, and pavement maze all within one acre.

I added an exclamation mark; but the printer has persistently omitted it. I often wonder what people expect. I should expect the worst; but I hope our visitors go home pleasantly surprised. As the garden is on such a small scale, it is very photogenic; but the camera lens flatters distance, and any person familiar with the garden through photographs must on visiting in person be surprised by the smallness of the scale, or hopefully charmed by its intimacy.

York Gate was purchased by my parents in 1951 when I was only seventeen years old. There was no garden as such with the house, and my father and mother began to lay it out, but from an early date I was given a fairly free hand to design and construct it. Although I had always had 'my garden' as a child I had no great experience, and had to make all the mistakes possible; but I learnt quickly. However all the garden has been remade at least once, and some parts twice or thrice.

From my earliest years I have had three abiding interests, gardening, design and collecting, and in the garden all these come together. I hope it means that an equal emphasis is placed upon the design and the planting of the garden.

Being a collector means that I not only collect plants (I constantly have to remind myself that I am not a botanic gardener) but I also collect garden ornaments. I find myself amazed how much ornament a garden can take, and yet when you look at the amount of furniture a room can absorb it is not perhaps so very surprising. I have to be very selective in my choice of ornament – no representations of the human form are allowed, although animals are permitted. However, nearly all the features are utilitarian things originally made for use – stone troughs and sinks, stone grinding wheels and mill stones, pump heads and old boilers, even large old kitchen pans. I feel these help to maintain the cottage garden atmosphere. I have yet satisfactorily to define in words the process by which I decide to place a particular object in a particular place.

When the companion volume, *The Englishwoman's Garden*, was published I was immensely struck by the brilliant photograph of the laburnum tunnel in Rosemary Verey's garden and tried to analyse the component parts of the picture. The tunnel is centred on what appears to be a pedestal sun dial, and if this is taken away the picture loses its point. I became aware that I had a vista with many similar component parts, but it lacked that essential focal point. By good fortune I was able to buy an old cast-iron pump which now forms the focal point of my vista. Look at Illustration 169, take the white pump head away, and you will see what I mean.

Over the past ten years I have been increasingly concerned with paving, and the laying of paving stones, stone setts, mill stones, cobbles, gravel in different sizes and granite setts in shades of dark grey, silver, buff and rose pink, and with forming different associations of these materials. It is interesting to note how over the same period our architects and planners have been showing a similar interest in the paving of the pedestrian ways of our city centres. I think we have to thank Japan for awakening our interest in this direction.

What of plants? My mother is a great reader of Margery

Fish, and for many years we have tried to be an 'all the year round garden'. We have planted for colour at either end of the season, and for obtaining two or hopefully three successions of bloom from the same patch of land. Bulbs are grown in profusion, and they mostly revel in our sandy, but hungry soil.

My current enthusiasms are for grasses, arums and aciphyllas. I find the names of grasses impossible to remember, and more than once have inadvertently ordered the same grass! I find they act as a splendid foil for all herbaceous plants. I have a root of the spiky grey *Helictotrichon sempervirens* planted where it can be viewed from my favourite seat, and I find the waving of the ever moving feathery plumes both therapeutic and relaxing.

I grow *Arum italicum* 'Pictum' in profusion, *A. creticum* with its splendid yellow flowers flourishes, but will not bloom; a recent addition is *A. dioscoridis* with a fleeting but attractively purple spotted spathe, and I have been honoured with a ghostly and ethereal flower from *A. orientalis*. The evil-looking and evil-smelling *Dracunculus vulgaris* flourishes well. *Arisarum proboscideum* is a show stopper for adults and children alike with its mouse-like flowers. *Arisaema candidissimum* usually produces its pink, white striped, curved and lipped funnels. *A. triphyllum*, the American Jack in the Pulpit, died after its first year; but *A. tortuosum*, which is of sensational appearance and which comes from India and is usually thought tender, has flowered regularly for the past six years. The supposedly hardy version of the florist's arum, *Zantedeschia aethiopica* 'Crowborough', will not establish itself.

165. View of the paved garden at the side of the house.

166. The white garden vista with the 'wobbly' column sundial.

167. View from the summerhouse down the yew-enclosed herb garden with box topiary.

168. The walk from the Dell to the raised canal in June.

169. The iris border in full bloom, leading to the so-called 'folly' with the white cast-iron pump head behind. Robin Spencer makes good use of material to create varying textures for his plants.

Aciphyllas are a race of New Zealand plants as yet rarely grown. They form rosettes of leaves, often spiky and dangerous, and vary in size from something nearly as large as a *Yucca* to something nearly as small as a *Sempervivum*. I grow them in scree conditions and find the genus fascinating.

I consider I am very lucky to be able to watch and tend what appears to be a comparatively mature garden which I have planted, and yet be only in comfortable middle age; but the creative process never stops, each year has its project, and the layout is still evolving.

By chance I owe Rosemary Verey another debt, for it was Arthur Hellyer who explained in the course of an article on her garden and apropos garden history that he considered the seventeenth century to be the age of making patterns, the eighteenth century the age of making pictures, the nineteenth century the age of the plant collector and the twentieth century the age of bringing all these facets into a harmonious whole. I think this crystallizes what has, firstly unconsciously and then consciously, been my aim and object.

Westend House, Wickwar, Gloucestershire

Keith Steadman's Garden

I started the garden at Westend House thirty years ago. It was my second garden and I was lucky enough to be able to leave behind all the mistakes and confusions of my first attempt and to start afresh.

I was fairly clear in my mind about a number of things, some positive some negative. I wanted, first and foremost, a natural garden, where what I planted could grow as it wished, where nature's inevitable change could be accommodated and not subverted; I wanted the final result to look as if it had happened naturally and had not been obviously contrived by man; I wanted it to be a continuous and related visual whole, to be looked at as an entity and not as a collection of individual plants; I wanted a garden of interest all the year round, and, perhaps most important of all, when it was mature it must demand the minimum of labour in upkeep.

I did not want the sort of garden which would take a few years to make and would then, for its yearly toll of labour, produce each year exactly the same result; I did not want a riot of colour or plants growing out of bare earth, as, apart from the fact that brown and green is a dismal colour scheme, I had no wish to spend a lot of my time weeding; I did not want velvet lawns demanding endless cosseting.

It was not going to be difficult to avoid the things which I did not want, but more of a problem to achieve those which I did.

The main area to be planted was a rectangle of roughly two acres, sloping gently to the west and surrounded on all sides by walls. A grass tennis court had been cut out of the natural slope, making a steep bank all along one side. At one end of this there was a Cedar of Lebanon, a Holm Oak, and an almost dead *Robinia*; at the other end, against the corner of the house, was a superb *Phillyrea latifolia*, the finest specimen that I have ever seen. So I had what was virtually an empty space in which to work.

I started by considering things in plan view and decided that I wanted one main open space with many smaller open areas linked by grass paths. I wanted that at any point there should be a choice of ways to go, as I felt strongly that the garden should be mysterious, not all seen at once, and should always hold out promise of more to be discovered round the next corner.

It was fairly easy to make a ground plan for the areas, which would have to be solidly planted in order to outline the open spaces. Although I realized that the shapes of these open spaces were important, it wasn't for many years, when the plants had grown and these areas were finally delineated, that I came to see that, visually, they were one of the most important things in the garden. Having settled in plan view the shape of what was in effect the framework, it was necessary to think about what trees and shrubs to use; at this point another dimension had to be considered, height, and this was a more difficult problem.

I walked round and round, visualizing the groups as if actually there, trying to decide the composition of each one, painting a landscape in my mind. There were so many things to be considered, the variation in height, shape and colour, the form of the plants in summer and winter, and the balance of evergreen to deciduous. It was while thinking about all this that I realized how important it was that every part of the garden should look right from whatever direction you approached it; this may seem obvious, but it is easy to think in one direction only, usually from the house outwards. The more I thought the more I was convinced that I wanted the garden to be a complete and continuous visual experience, that one part should lead naturally to another without any marked transition of mood, and to achieve this I knew that it would all have to be carefully thought out. At all costs I wanted to avoid the situation where plants, however beautiful, had so little visual relation to one another that the only way to look at them was one at a time.

Having finally decided what trees and shrubs should form the framework I set to and planted them. And there they were. Groups of small plants in an expanse of rough grass, meaningless to anyone but myself. So they remained for years, until they had grown together enough to show up the shapes of the open spaces which they surrounded. While the plants were small and the whole design apparently formless, I found that the shapes of the future open spaces could be shown up by cutting the grass there much shorter than in the planted areas. This at once made the plan of the garden visible, and was a great help in the next stage of the planting. In the following years I had great pleasure in building up the main planting against this background. I spent a lot of time looking at trees and shrubs in gardens, nurseries and the

170. A mass of *Philadelphus* in the white garden.

arboretum at Westonbirt, providentially only a dozen miles away, and while doing this I learnt a great deal, not only about trees and shrubs but also about how to use them in relation to one another, to make the effects that I wanted.

Over the years, working to this idea, I have acquired many unusual and little-used plants, but I now realize that this sort of garden can be made with quite commonly planted trees and shrubs and still be just as beautiful; it is the way in which they are used in relation to one another, the balance of colour, texture and form, which is the important thing.

From this it will be clear that, while deeply interested in plants, I am not a collector. I am not interested in plants simply because they are rare and mere possession brings me no satisfaction at all.

When I began I had little knowledge of how to achieve my aims, other than a firm conviction about the basic idea. I had no real understanding how to proceed. Everything I have done to fill out my original conception has been learned along the way and I have enjoyed it immensely.

In thirty years of planting obviously there have been failures: *Cornus florida rubra* which never flowered, liquidambars which stayed stubbornly green in autumn, so-called ground cover which usually didn't, *Cladrastis sinensis* which took twenty years to flower and then did it while I was away, and has never done it since, and many more. Whenever any plant has failed to satisfy me I have always hardened my heart and got rid of it. But as well as the failures there have been successes. A fine *Cornus controversa* 'Variegata', on its own roots and growing beautifully, the marvellously exuberant hybrid wingnut *Pterocarya rehderiana* with its multitudes of pale lime-green winged fruits in hanging tassels, a great many willows with their lovely catkins of many different colours, the deciduous *Elaeagnus umbellata parvifolia* which scents the whole garden in spring, the much neglected family of privets, especially *Ligustrum lucidum*, and best of all to me, a lovely rose, the reward of untidiness, as the seedling was allowed to germinate between some paving stones. It has lovely grey leaves and thousands of small sweetly scented white flowers, and it will climb to twenty feet; one of its parents I am sure is the Himalayan Musk Rose *Rosa brunonii*. These and very many more give me delight each day throughout the year.

I think that if I had started with the knowledge and experience which I now have I might have made a better garden, but it would have been far less rewarding.

In most respects I now have the sort of garden which I set out to make and in maturity it brings me more pleasure than I could possibly have foreseen.

Keith Steadman

171. Gorse and *Prunus* 'Tai Haku' and other shrubs are allowed to grow unhindered.

172. A fine specimen of *Cornus controversa* 'Variegata'.

173. Part of the vast Himalayan Musk Rose *Rosa brunonii* and its seedling, now named *Rosa* 'Wickwar'.

174. Giant Umbellifers and other plants create a jungle effect around a garden feature made from the cast-iron balconies of demolished Georgian houses.

Briar Cottage, Horsell, Surrey

Graham Thomas's Garden

Having enjoyed an acre of garden for twenty-five years I decided to move into something smaller six years ago; this short account outlines the initial considerations and gives a sketch of the planting. It is difficult not to be complacent and enthusiastic; in a space of six years failures and mistakes are not too evident. It is amazing how in a mere quarter of an acre so many plants from all over the world will grow. The land falls slightly from south to north and the soil is acid, well drained, but fairly retentive.

Before doing any planting, it is necessary to examine down-pipes and know the positions of rain-water sumps; also to examine fence-posts and resolve to plant nothing shrubby near them in case they need struts in the future. The garden needed clearing out; cherries were pushing up the paving and low front wall, shrubs of poor quality abounded and there were no less than three Bramley's Seedling apple which I reduced to one. Another tree proved to be an early culinary variety and this has been grafted with several dessert apples.

Although the garden has great trees not far away, there was a need for a few small ones in the front garden, placed so that they would obscure a neighbour's house but not shade the planting space. I chose the ferny-leafed evergreen *Nothofagus menziesii, Prunus subhirtella* 'Autumnalis Rosea' and *Koelreuteria paniculata*. The front garden, a narrow strip, has a new path, paved, dividing the plot, which is about twenty-four feet by eighty, into four long beds. The bungalow faces north-east, so that the two beds under the walls are cool and shady after midday, and suitable for hellebores, ferns, winter-flowering rhododendrons, sarcococcas, *Aucuba japonica* 'Sulphurea' (cream-edged, not spotted), cyclamens and snowdrops. The assortment indicates winter interest, and this is what the front garden is devoted to; one is able to enjoy the winter flowers without entering the main garden. The two sunnier plots contain *Viburnum farreri, Rhododendron* 'Nobleanum Venustum', *Hamamelis* 'Pallida' and *Skimmia* 'Rubella', the last showing red-brown buds all the winter. Adding to the floral display are shrubs for leaf and twig colour, such as *Elaeagnus × ebbingei* 'Gilt Edge', the best red-twigged Dogwood, *Cornus alba* 'Sibirica', *Mahonia aquifolium* 'Moseri', whose leaves are a soft coral red through the winter, the clear greens of *Hebe rakaiensis* and *Helleborus corsicus*. These all make a varied background to drifts of lowly planting, mainly *Erica herbacea* (*E. carnea*) mounding up on the shrubby sides with *E. × darleyensis* forms. For variety are prostrate junipers and *Microbiota decussata, Hebe pinquifolia* 'Pagei' and *Iris foetidissima* 'Variegata', and to lighten the whole mass, clumps of grey *Festuca glauca*. On the low boundary wall are established compact and colourful forms of ivy. In time the most bulky plant, though slow-growing, will be *Rhododendron ponticum* 'Foliis Purpureis', whose leaves, green in summer, turn to the colour of a Copper Beech in winter. Along the verges are various choice snowdrops, early-flowering scillas, crocuses, daffodils and irises of the *reticulata* group, all contributing their quota from November to March, weather permitting!

The main garden is about sixty feet by eighty, with two extra recessed areas, paved and bordered, where the garden doors debouch. These provide sitting places for the later part of the day, being shaded by the house in the mornings. I believe a garden should contain several 'garden rooms' for sitting and taking meals, preferably in the sun; there was again the need to place small trees or tall shrubs to blot out neighbouring houses and provide greenery all around, without casting shade on the sitting places. The rootiest, shadiest far left corner was reserved for compost and bonfires screened by trellis and climbers, the other for making a sunk garden, providing the only place for breakfast in the sun.

After coming round the house, through the side gate on to the paved court, there is a broad step up; from this a long broad strip of grass – one cannot call it a lawn – curves away past the compost corner, leading down two steps into the sunk garden. The verges of the grass are paved, allowing plants to flop forward, and provide dry access in winter; all other paths are paved. The first corner is warm and sunny all round except on one side where there is coolness and moisture. An established *Elaeagnus pungens* 'Maculata' and the reddish walls of the bungalow dictated the colour scheme for this part and the two main borders flanking the grass: yellow, white, blue and purple flowers supplemented by the yellow-leafed *Ribes sanguineum* 'Brocklebankii', glaucous-leafed things like rue, and coppery *Ajuga reptans* 'Atropurpurea'. The display starts in spring with various tiny bulbs along the verges, covered over by *Viola* 'Huntercombe Purple' and other small things later.

In the warmest corner are *Carpenteria californica, Hypericum chinense, Salvia patens, Zantedeschia* (Arum) in four hardy forms including 'Green Goddess', all contributing to the colour scheme, and two forms of the November-flowering scented *Camellia sasanqua*.

In June the lavender *Iris missouriensis* and yellow *I. kerneriana* flower, backed by *Campanula latiloba* 'Alba', *Geranium* 'Johnson's Blue', *Hemerocallis flava* – very fragrant, canary yellow – and Rose 'Nevada'. Later other yellow fragrant Day Lilies take over, together with *Hypericum kouytchense* (which I place first among shrubby kinds), Roses 'Golden Wings' and 'Roseraie de l'Haÿ'; lavender blue *Clematis* 'Xerxes' on the fence, which it shares with *C. viticella* 'Elegans Plena' in murrey-purple for August; while *Aster × frikartii* 'Mönch' starts its three-month display of classy lavender-blue daisies against the creamy white of *Hydrangea arborescens* 'Grandiflora' and, later, *H. paniculata* 'Tardiva'. For August and September there are various Montbretias, *Hibiscus syriacus* 'Blue Bird', *Gentiana asclepiadea*, and *Anemone × hybrida* 'Honorine Jobert', the incomparable white Japanese Anemone.

The bend of the grass brings us to a fairly cool border on the left backed by a grey fence on which are honeysuckles and pink and white clematises. Here are *Rhododendron* 'Damaris Logan', light yellow, 'Vanessa Pastel' and *R. yakushimanum*, and early and late flowering azaleas together with that most beautiful of all camellias, *C. × williamsii* 'J.C. Williams' in light pink. Various trilliums, epimediums, Solomon's Seal (*Polygonatum*), hardy orchids (*Dactylorrhiza*), Lionel Fortescue's exquisite *Primula* 'Devon Cream', a giant oxlip in effect, and the choicer hostas. Later interest is provided by the tiny pale blue *Hydrangea serrata thunbergii* and sweet-scented *Clethra tomentosa*.

The middle portion of the garden is being built up with shrubs so that in due course one will not see round the bend of the grass walk. There are many of the older roses, but two principal shrubs are *Magnolia* 'Maryland', which is a compact early-flowering hybrid of *M. grandiflora*, and the September-flowering *Ligustrum quihoui*. Most of the roses are Bourbons and Portlands, thus giving me a succession of button-holes to wear. One corner is devoted to *Perovskia* 'Blue Spire' growing through a carpet of *Polygonum affine* 'Superbum'. Pinks and silvery foliage plants flop onto the paved paths. Colchicums assort well with this colour scheme in September.

The sunk garden not only provides a place for breakfast, but its stepped retaining walls are a home for alpine plants. The soil on the shady side was mixed with peat, and the sunny ledges mixed with old mortar and grit. Several dozen dwarf plants were chosen to provide interest from March to September. *Fuchsia magellanica* 'Prostrata' flowers nobly for weeks, likewise the pale pink, black-eyed flowers of *Erodium brownhowi*. The sunk garden is paved; in it purple alyssum (*Lobularia maritima*) seeds itself to contrast with a large pot of *Pelargonium* 'The Boar' in soft salmon which is stood near to the round stone table in front of the seat.

Behind the seat is another trellis screen covered with the fragrant large-leafed *Hedera colchica*, honeysuckle, *Rosa wichuraiana* for August and the magnificent violet-blue *Clematis × durandii*, a herbaceous plant which has growing through it another, the coral-red pea *Lathyrus rotundifolius*.

175. A corner of the house looking from the main garden in spring. *Elaeagnus pungens* 'Maculata', *Ribes sanguineum* 'Pulborough Scarlet', *Euphorbia characias wulfenii* and in the foreground, *E. myrsinites* are much in evidence.

176. A detail of the retaining wall in the sunk garden. From right to left *Campanula betulifolia*, *Hypericum olympicum* 'Citrinum' and *Erodium supracanum*.

177. *Clematis alpina* in April.

The path leads back to the side door and tea-sitting corner, through an arch covered with the excellent full-flavoured blackberry 'Oregon Thornless'; the path dividing the vegetable patch from the rest of the garden is flanked by pairs of standard roses – among which are pink 'Ballerina' and 'Little White Pet'; the third is yet to be found. The path leads to the grand glaucous foliage of Seakale, various herbs, *Rosa stellata mirifica* and artemisias while on the south-west wall of the house are nerines, *Lathyrus nervosus* or Lord Anson's Blue Pea, and *Iris unguicularis* forms. On the north-west wall are Winter Jasmine and the intensely fragrant white Japanese Apricot, *Prunus mume* 'Omoi-no-mama', which opens in February.

I have only mentioned a few of the plants I grow, though it has been rather a long list. Apart from periods of intense frost there is always something in flower. It is a labour-saving garden where full use is made of ground-cover plants and stalwarts like phloxes, Bearded Irises, lavenders and *Agapanthus*; spare ground is covered by a mulch of leaves or sterile compost or peat, thus limiting weeding to the minimum. There are no hedges to clip, and when the shrubs and plants become fully established there will be more time available for sitting on the seats.

Graham Thomas

178. The path along the front of the bungalow in late February with varieties of *Erica herbacea* and *E.* × *darleyensis*, *Elaeagnus* × *ebbingei* 'Gilt Edge', *Hebe pinguifolia* 'Pagei' on the right and *Rhododendron* Cilpinense, 'Christmas Cheer' and *Carex morrowii* 'Variegata' on the left.

179. The main garden in June. Four years after planting, *Geranium* 'Johnson's Blue', *Hemerocallis flava* and *Ribes sanguineum* 'Brocklebankii' on the left and on the right *Alchemilla mollis*, *Iris pallida dalmatica*, *Papaver orientale* and *Lilium pyrenaicum* 'Rubrum' are well established.

Burford House, Tenbury Wells, Worcestershire

John Treasure's Garden

The River Teme, on its journey from central Wales, flows below the walls of Ludlow Castle, a one-time stronghold of the great Mortimer lordship. Some ten miles downstream its northern bank is joined by the deeply cut Ledwych brook. Brook and river form the south and west boundaries of the grounds to Burford House, once another Mortimer residence, and which before the Mortimers was a Saxon fortress. In 1304 Hugh de Mortimer married a Cornwall, and thereafter the Cornwall barons ruled supreme, until 1721, when, presumably, a decaying castle was sold to William Bowles. In 1726 Bowles built the present house on the old site, a fine well-proportioned brick building. Much later, two poorly designed Victorian wings were added.

Ever since designing my first garden (one mile from Burford House), it was my brother's and my ambition to create a garden for the public to see plants growing in natural surroundings, and a nursery adjoining where those plants could be purchased.

In 1953 Burford came up for sale with its eighteen acres of land. My brother and I, on a cold, wet February morning, inspected the property with a view to purchasing. We liked what we saw and decided to make an offer. It was not until April 1954 that the contract was signed and Burford was ours. That April work was immediately started on the house. The two Victorian wings were removed and Bowles' house converted into two flats.

To the north, south and west there were some four acres of grounds. A garden was virtually non-existent. On the north front, beyond the carriage drive, was a fine lawn leading up to a large rectangular moat – at each end a fine London Plane (*Platanus acerifolia*) and nearby a magnificent Copper Beech. East of the house was a vast complex of buildings, and nearly all of these had to be demolished. Two small houses were later built on the area. To the south, an uneven four-foot path against the house, and beyond an immense lawn leading to the boundary ha-ha. Here there stood on one side a fine old *Pinus nigra* and on the east side a tall Wellingtonia (*Sequoiadendron giganteum*). To the east of this lawn was an old apple orchard, partly walled with a line of Scotch Firs and other conifers forming the east and south boundary. One good feature was a very large, old English Yew (*Taxus baccata*).

River and brook form the boundary on the west side, and here was mostly 'meadow' – the only feature being a semi-circle of tall, miserable conifers opposite the house, where, I was told, the servants in past days hung out the washing! The conifers were removed, and later I designed a semi-formal garden instead – now named the 'Summer Garden'.

While waiting for the contract to be signed, I took the risk of making a survey and preparing a plan. The land was flat except on the south and west fronts, where levels had to be taken. But I knew what I wanted: formality on these two fronts, and for formality to quickly break down to the informal. While work on the house was in progress I used labour to achieve the formal effect. A terrace was formed on the south front, steps and dwarf walls constructed and the ground levelled to form small lawns. On the west end I left three walls of the Victorian wing standing at a height of six feet, so making an enclosed patio with a central pool. This is now the Courtyard Garden, and brick steps lead down from it to the formal west lawn and the Summer Garden beyond.

For informality I wanted spaciousness, surprise views and a sense that the garden would appear to be much larger than its actual size. For this effect I retained large areas of lawn, planned new lawns alongside river and brook, and formed a stream in the west part, now known as the 'Stream Garden'. I planned curving borders in front of walls and at the edge of the Teme and its tributary and designed large island beds.

180. The attractive red-brick house, built in 1726, is now enhanced by John Treasure's formal planting. Urns overflow with ivy-leaf geraniums; *Wisteria* and *Carpenteria* clothe the walls.

These beds of abstract shape with deep curves and promontories appear to increase the size of a garden. 'Secrecy' is obtained and the positioning of plants enhanced.

During 1955 the two large island beds with deep bays and projections were shaped on the south lawn. Between these beds a 'valley of lawn' extending the full length of the original lawn was thus created. Two more large island borders in the Stream Garden were also formed.

It was not until the mid-sixties that I planned more of these beds in the old apple orchard, another stream and large areas of grass. No planning was necessary on the north side. It was not until 1966 that the 'Fountain Pool', set in the middle of the lawn and central to the house, was added.

I commenced planting as soon as borders were shaped. Flooding in the early years was a perpetual nightmare – floods occurred frequently. Today they rarely happen. Anticipation causes most distress, but floods have their advantage – they deposit good soil. I had soil tests taken throughout the garden and the pH was 7.9. Nevertheless, wanting to grow ericaceous plants, I tried a few with success! *Rhododendron* 'Blue Diamond' is now seven feet high!

Today, after twenty-eight years, the garden has grown up. I have planted trees and shrubs as isolated subjects on the lawns – *Liriodendron tulipifera, Acer saccharinum, Magnolia hypoleuca, Parrotia persica, Nyssa sylvatica* – and these just a few among many. Single conifers and conifers in groups play their part on the lawns too. Happily *Torreya californica* has not succumbed to severe winters, as I was told it might.

Trees and shrubs also add to the attraction of the island borders. The trees give a tall spinal effect, the shrubs a 'build up' to the trees. Herbaceous plants fill the gaps between the shrubs. I found it nearly impossible to place the latter until the right 'atmosphere' and protection had been created by the taller-growing subjects. Acers and birches (*Betula*), *Amelanchier* and *Prunus, Cornus* species, magnolias, *Eucryphia, Cercidiphyllum japonicum* are only some of the taller growers and among shrubs; then *Philadelphus*, deutzias, viburnums, hydrangeas, *Potentilla, Hamamelis mollis* and other winter flowers – again only a few among many. Not only in the island beds, but also in other borders does this pattern of planting occur. In the spaces between shrubs I have used many and varied herbaceous plants. For example to mention several, *Helleborus* and ferns, many different hostas, cardiocrinums, various *Meconopsis* species, the beautiful pale blue *Glaucidium palmatum*, veratrums, *Paeonia, Dianthus*, helianthemums, and many grey and silver foliage plants. In the island borders, particularly in the east garden (the old apple orchard), this has created an almost woodland effect.

145

I have found streamside planting exciting, but very hard work. Moisture-loving plants grow very fast. Some of the plants flourishing beside the two streams include astilbes, several species of *Iris*, primulas, rodgersias, *Senecio smithii*, *Rheum palmatum*, and the handsome *Arundo donax*, which has survived many winters as has *Schizostylis* 'Sunrise', surprisingly growing in a few inches of water – at times frozen solid and under ice. I have found that *Schizostylis* 'Mrs Hegarty' makes a pleasing picture growing around the white-stemmed willow, *Salix irrorata*.

On walls in the east garden and on the house, climbers and shrubs add to the effect. *Wisteria floribunda macrobotrys* with its long mauve-blue racemes makes a wonderful display in spring. *Clematis* 'Daniel Deronda' climbs through *Robinia kelseyi*, Rose 'Madame Alfred Carrière' plays host to *Clematis* 'Sir Garnet Wolseley'. *Carpenteria californica* is now a fine plant by the south door. *Rosa sinowilsonii* has survived many winters, so too *Fremontodendron* 'California Glory'. Deep-blue *Ceanothus* 'Italian Skies', and the pink double-flowered *Clematis* 'Proteus', look well together.

I grow some 130 *Clematis* species and hybrids in the garden. Many losses occurred in the early years owing to wilt, but now home production has almost stopped this disease. *Clematis* climb through flowering shrubs into trees, and I train them on the ground through low-growing plants. I had (and still have) great affection for *Clematis* in the early years, but affection changed as my gardening experience extended. Roses came next, and now it is herbaceous plants and ferns!

Of roses I only cultivate the Chinas and the 'Old Roses'. They look well in the summer garden mixed with *Delphinium*, *Phlox*, penstemons, *Eryngium*, *Verbascum*, *Aconitum* and many other plants.

Of course I have had many failures over the years. Hundreds of discarded labels (I label every plant) testify to this, but then this is all part of gardening!

I opened the gardens to the public in the spring of 1959. Visitors have been kind and complimentary and given me encouragement, a sense of achievement and of happiness – but can a gardener ever feel fulfilled and appreciate the magic of his own creation?

John Treasure.

181. Astilbes, willows, ferns and contrasting leaf effects carpet the banks of the streams.

182. John Treasure's aim has been to achieve a smooth transition from formal to informal, by using shrubs, flowering trees and upright evergreens in island beds. His large areas of lawn give an impression of spaciousness.

183. A garden with a feeling of maturity yet there are always new plantings and colour effects to enjoy.

184. An enviable feature of this immaculate garden is the River Teme. The course is emphasized by imaginative planting.

Biographical Notes

HARDY AMIES is the founder of an *haute couture* house in London. He is one of the Dressmakers by Appointment to the Queen, who has made him a Commander of the Royal Victorian Order. He has an international reputation as a designer of clothes for men.

SIR FREDERICK ASHTON, O.M., C.H., was born in Ecuador in 1904. He is Founder Choreographer of the Royal Ballet.

BILL BAKER is a retired dental surgeon who has always been interested in plants, even sending seed home from North Africa and Italy during the war. Plant-hunting holidays have taken him three times to Russia, to north-west Africa, Turkey and the Atlas Mountains, although Greece and the Mediterranean islands remain his favourite area. He is treasurer of the R.H.S. lily group.

LAWRENCE BANKS is the fourth generation of his family to garden at Hergest. He is active in many organizations concerned with the preservation of our unique English gardening heritage and is chairman of the National Council for the Conservation of Plants and Gardens. In between times he is a merchant banker.

EGBERT BARNES was born in 1898, educated at Winchester, served in the Royal Artillery in the First World War and was admitted solicitor in 1928. For many years he was chairman of the family brewery and wine merchanting company. His main interests are fishing, wine, picture collecting and working in his garden, which he enjoys at all seasons of the year.

JEREMY BENSON is an architect practising from Walpole House. He is much involved in the repair of historic buildings and with the national amenities organization. He is chairman of the Georgian Group.

VISCOUNT BLAKENHAM served as an Alderman on London County Council in 1937–52, in the Suffolk Yeomanry during the Second World War and as a member of Parliament from 1945 to 1963. He was successively Secretary of State for War (1956–8), Minister of Agriculture (1958–60) and Minister of Labour (1960–63). He was treasurer of the Royal Horticultural Society in 1970–81 and chairman of the National Trust Gardens Panel. He died in March 1982.

JOHN CODRINGTON was born in 1898, educated at Harrow, Sandhurst and Oxford and served with the Coldstream Guards from 1917 for twenty years and in the Intelligence Corps during the Second World War. After nine years with Sir Alexander Korda's film company he became a garden designer, mainly in the British Isles but with a practice embracing many out-of-the-way places, including Timbuktu.

LORD DE RAMSEY was appointed H.M. Lieutenant for the County of Huntingdon after war service which included being a prisoner of war in the Far East. He was appointed to Huntingdon and Peterborough from 1965 to 1968 and has been Deputy Lieutenant for Cambridge since 1974.

RALPH DUTTON, F.S.A., was born in 1898. He has been a trustee of the Wallace Collection and a member of the Historic Buildings Council and of several National Trust committees. He is author of *The English Country House, The English Garden, The Châteaux of France* etc.

FRANCIS EGERTON, M.C., was born in 1918 and educated at Eton and Christ Church, Oxford. He is chairman of Mallet and Son (Antiques) at 40 New Bond Street.

JOE ELLIOTT trained at the Royal Botanic Garden, Edinburgh, with two six-month breaks – to build a rock garden in India for the Maharajah of Jaipur and for a spell at the New York Botanic Gardens. In 1946 he started Broadwell Nurseries, specializing in alpines and other interesting and unusual hardy plants. He is a member of the council of the Royal Horticultural Society, has served on the Alpine Garden Society and written *Alpines in Sinks and Troughs*, published by that society.

LIONEL FORTESCUE was born in 1892, the son of W. B. Fortescue, the landscape artist of the Newlyn School. After Blundells, Oxford, service in the First World War and political work in Persia, in 1923 he joined the staff of Eton from where he retired early, in 1945, moved to Devon and devoted the rest of his life to the creation of the Garden House. He died in July 1981.

SIR FREDERICK GIBBERD practises architecture, town design and landscape architecture. He is the only architect to have designed a cathedral, a mosque and a non-conformist chapel. Other buildings by him are London Airport and Coutts Bank in the Strand. Over the last thirty-five years he has been responsible for the design of the new town of Harlow, in which his garden is situated. As a landscape architect his designs include reservoirs, pumping and power stations and a mine.

PETER HEALING served with the Royal Artillery during the war and now lives in Gloucestershire, where he is a magistrate.

HUGH JOHNSON is a Jekyll and Hyde character, known to gardeners as the Editorial Director of *The Garden* and *The Plantsman*, as 'Tradescant' of the monthly diary and as author of *The Principles of Gardening* and *The International Book of Trees*. His darker side is writing about wine: *The World Atlas of Wine* and his annual *Pocket Wine Book*.

LORD LAMBTON was a Member of Parliament from 1951 to 1973. He served as Principle Private Secretary to the Minister of Defence and to the Foreign Secretary in 1955–7, but resigned at the time of Suez. He was Secretary for Air from 1970 to 1973.

JOHN LAST is a marine biologist and a wildlife artist. Roger Last works in television production and is a writer and broadcaster. Both are founder members of the Norfolk Churches Trust.

FRANK LAWLEY was born in Staffordshire, studied painting with Victor Pasmore and Harry Turner and taught at Newcastle Art School. A fortunate meeting with Graham Thomas turned his life decisively towards gardening and the establishment of a nursery.

CHRISTOPHER LLOYD divides his time between horticultural journalism and running the gardens and nursery for unusual plants at Great Dixter. He has contributed the weekly 'In My Garden' column for *Country Life* for twenty years and also writes regularly for *Popular Gardening*, the *Observer Magazine* and the *Guardian*. His best-known book is *The Well-Tempered Garden*.

SIR BERNARD LOVELL, F.R.S., was born in Gloucestershire and first went to Manchester as a member of the University Physics Department in 1936. He returned there after war service and founded the Jodrell Bank radio-astronomy observatory, which he directed until his retirement in 1981.

DAVID MCCLINTOCK is the author or co-author of various books, including *The Pocket Guide to Wild Flowers* (1956) and *Companion to Flowers* (1966), and numerous articles. He is past president of the Botanical Society of the British Isles and a member of the Scientific and Publication committees of the R.H.S. He was recently awarded the Veitch Memorial Medal by the R.H.S.

MAURICE MASON was born in Fincham in 1912 and has lived there ever since. An ever-increasing affection for plants, tender and hardy, led him over the years to build up what must be one of the largest collections in private hands in England.

BEVERLEY NICHOLS published his first novel at the age of nineteen, over sixty years ago. Since then he has produced some seventy volumes of novels, fantasies, plays and autobiographies, of which the most famous is *Down the Garden Path*.

FRED NUTBEAM has spent a life's work in horticulture in some of the stately homes of Britain. After war service in the navy he was appointed Head Gardener at St Donat's Castle (1946–53) and from 1954 until his retirement in 1978 he was head of the Royal Gardens at Buckingham Palace.

NICHOLAS RIDLEY trained as a civil engineer but after eight years of practice went into politics. After various vicissitudes on both back and front benches in Government and in Opposition, he became Financial Secretary to the Treasury in September 1981.

MARK RUMARY is a landscape designer who trained originally as an architect. He has created many gardens, not only in the British Isles, but also in Europe and the Middle East. A director of Notcutts Landscape Limited, he has been responsible for several years for designing Notcutts exhibits at the Chelsea Flower Show which have won many awards from the R.H.S., including the Lawrence Medal for the best exhibit of the year.

SIR DAVID SCOTT was born in 1887, joined the Foreign Office in 1911 and retired in 1947. With his second wife, Valerie Finnis, whom he married in 1970, he spends his time gardening and looking at gardens.

DR JAMES SMART qualified in medicine at St Thomas's Hospital in 1937. After war service in the Navy as a Surgeon Lieutenant Commander he practised in Barnstaple as an anaesthetist, retiring in 1976. He has since spent two months of each winter in Australia, seeing and collecting plants. He is on the Rhododendron and Camellia Committees of the R.H.S., director of the International Camellia Society and a member of the International Dendrology Society and the Garden Society.

ROBIN SPENCER lived all his life in Leeds and was a chartered surveyor by profession. He was a bachelor and gardened York Gate without any outside help but with much assistance from his mother. He died in May 1982.

KEITH STEADMAN has been a keen gardener for over thirty years. On retirement from his business ten years ago he took to propagating and selling some of his rarer plants, which had become unobtainable, and now has a thriving small nursery.

GRAHAM THOMAS trained at the University Botanic Garden, Cambridge, and is now Gardens Consultant to the National Trust. Both photographer and artist, he is well known as a writer and lecturer and is world-famous for his work in gathering and popularizing old and new shrub roses. He has been awarded the Veitch Memorial Medal and the Victoria Medal of Honour by the R.H.S., the Dean Hole Medal by the Royal National Rose Society and the O.B.E., for his work with the National Trust. He is a vice-president of the Garden History Society and of the Royal National Rose Society. He is the author of nine books on plants and gardens.

JOHN TREASURE was born in Shropshire and trained as an architect. A growing interest in horticulture led to one ambition – to create a garden for his own satisfaction and for others.

Acknowledgements

The photographs in this book were taken by: Bill Baker, 11–15; Peter Coates, 52–5; *Cheshire Life*, 112; Richard Dormer, 27–31; Joe Elliott, 64, 67; Valerie Finnis, 38–51, 54, 65, 108, 153–8; Sir Frederick Gibberd, 74–9; Jerry Harpur, 21–6, 96–100, 128–34, 147–52, 165, 167; Peter Healing, title page; John Holroyd, 166, 168, 169; Hugh Johnson, 85–90; Lucinda Lambton, 91–5; Roger Last, 98; Frank Lawley, 101–6; Georges Lévêque, 3; Sir Bernard Lovell, 113–16; Derry Moore, 7, 10; R. H. M. Robinson of the Harry Smith Horticultural Photographic Collection, 5, 6, 8, 9, 32–7, 62–3, 66; John Rodgers, 117–21, 135–40; Dr James Smart, 159–64; Graham Thomas, 175–9; Pamla Toler, end pages, 1, 2, 4, 16–20, 56–61, 80–84, 107, 110, 141–6, 170–74; Michael Warren, 109, 111, 122–7, 180–84; Keith Wiley, 68–73. The photograph on page 14 is by Jerry Harpur.

The drawings at the openings of the articles are by Davina Wynne Jones of Gryffon Publications (pp. 16, 24, 40, 52, 60, 64, 72, 76, 80, 84, 100, 108, 116), Laurie Clark (pp. 20, 28, 32, 36, 44, 48, 56, 88, 92, 96, 104, 112, 120, 128, 132, 136, 140, 144) and Sir Frederick Gibberd (p. 68).

Index

References in the text to individual plants are included only where cultivation hints or details are given. Page numbers in italics refer to illustrations.